Penguin Masterstudies

Henry V

William Tydeman is Professor of English at the University College of North Wales, where he has taught since leaving Oxford University in 1961. His publications include *The Theatre in the Middle Ages* (1978), *Doctor Faustus: Text and Performance* (1984) and *English Medieval Theatre 1400–1500* (1986). Among the works he has edited are *Plays* by Tom Robertson (1982), the Casebook on Oscar Wilde's comedies (1982) and *Four Tudor Comedies* for Penguin Books in 1984. His leisure interests include directing and performing in plays.

Penguin Masterstudies
Joint Advisory Editors
Stephen Coote and Bryan Loughrey

William Shakespeare
Henry V

William Tydeman

Penguin Books

Penguin Books Ltd, Harmondsworth, Middlesex, England
Viking Penguin Inc., 40 West 23rd Street, New York, New York 10010, USA
Penguin Books Australia Ltd, Ringwood, Victoria, Australia
Penguin Books Canada Ltd, 2801 John Street, Markham, Ontario, Canada L3R 1B4
Penguin Books (NZ) Ltd, 182–190 Wairau Road, Auckland 10, New Zealand

First published 1987

Copyright © William Tydeman, 1987
All rights reserved

Filmset in Monophoto Times
Made and printed in Great Britain by
Richard Clay Ltd, Bungay, Suffolk

Except in the United States of America, this book is sold subject to
the condition that it shall not, by way of trade or otherwise, be lent,
re-sold, hired out, or otherwise circulated without the publisher's
prior consent in any form of binding or cover other than that in
which it is published and without a similar condition including this
condition being imposed on the subsequent purchaser

Contents

Introduction	7
History and the Elizabethans	15
The Man and the Myth	23
Henry in the Playhouse	40
Shakespeare and War	50
Henry V: Text	61
Structure	64
Language	75
Characterization	89
Themes	108
The Play in the Theatre	120
Conclusion	134
Further Reading	139

Introduction

It was from Laurence Olivier's film version, released in 1945, that I formed my first impressions of Shakespeare's *Henry V*. Still at primary school, alternately besotted with the valorous deeds of Robin Hood and those of the Dambusters, I was taken one half-term afternoon to the local cinema, a special enough treat to warrant my mother buying us seats amid the lush plush of the dress circle. Relief at the Allied victory in Europe being all-pervasive at the time, the patriotic preliminaries to the screening included a performance of the *Trumpet Voluntary* on the Mighty Wurlitzer, or whatever breed of organ passed for its Kentish equivalent. Once the velvety darkness descended and the film began, I sat enraptured, spellbound by the breezy charm of the yellow-sashed Chorus, the Dauphin's derisory gift of tennis balls, the haunted face of the dying Falstaff, the glow of the watch-fires and the 'whip-whip' of the arrows through the Agincourt air, the detritus of the war-torn French countryside. I relished the glimpses backstage at the Globe playhouse, the cardboard-cut-out-style settings for the French court, the heady spectacle of the battle itself. But above all, it was the titular soldier-king who captured my imagination and supplied the pattern for solo acting-games for most of the coming summer holidays; resolute, self-reliant, energetic, modest, cheerful in danger, generous in victory, Shakespeare's hero appeared as the epitome of that national spirit which had so recently been successfully invoked when Britain stood alone against Adolf Hitler and survived to help remove the scourge of Nazism from the face of Europe.

> Upon his royal face there is no note
> How dread an army hath enrounded him,
> Nor doth he dedicate one jot of colour
> Unto the weary and all-watchèd night,
> But freshly looks, and overbears attaint
> With cheerful semblance and sweet majesty;
> That every wretch, pining and pale before,
> Beholding him, plucks comfort from his looks.

As I shinned up trees in the garden, urging my imaginary troops once more unto the breach, or assured the cat that everything depended upon the king, Henry V reigned for me as my ideal English monarch, while the work bearing his name did duty even longer as 'My Favourite Play'.

Masterstudies: Henry V

Forty years on, I am inclined to be critical of my taste both in Elizabethan drama and in British sovereigns, yet K. B. McFarlane, a most judicious medieval historian, has nominated Henry as 'the greatest man that ever ruled England' (*Lancastrian Kings and Lollard Knights*), while Ronald Berman felt able to introduce his *Twentieth-Century Interpretations of 'Henry V'* by speaking of Shakespeare's 'very considerable accomplishment' in unifying within this play the matter of epic and that of history, and so creating one satisfying whole. Perhaps a ten-year-old's judgement is not to be dismissed as utterly unsound.

However, it is scarcely difficult to avoid dissenting from scholarly experts and play-acting schoolboys in one's estimation of both king and drama. Henry may have represented the acme of regal excellence for Lancastrian and Tudor chroniclers in their day, and at the time of Olivier's film he may have appealed (even to more sophisticated tastes than mine) as the embodiment of all those traits the British believe they exemplify on occasions of national crisis (some Conservative politician doubtless quoted from one of Henry's martial speeches during the late, lamented Falklands conflict). But there has been no shortage of historians in the past few decades who voiced reservations on the subject of Henry's true character and achievements, just as there has been no dearth of literary critics who find Shakespeare's 'warlike Harry' unworthy of his creator's attention, let alone his approval. Even those who argue that we should judge the king by the standards of the fifteenth century rather than those of our own seem unable to accord him their unqualified approbation, while those who claim to appreciate Shakespeare's motives for apparently endorsing the moral worth of Henry's military valour often argue that as a piece of theatre *Henry V* lacks either the warmth or the depth of its author's more sophisticated or engaging products.

In the latter part of our own century this line of criticism has naturally gained strength from a growing public distaste for the notions of war and conquest; we are no longer much impressed by national leaders who employ 'famine, sword and fire' to gain their ends. The global stakes are now felt to be too high to sanction this kind of aggressive posturing, and we shy away from Shakespeare's ostensible glorification of it. Often regarded as his least interesting and least coherent history drama outside the three parts of *Henry VI*, the play has been increasingly liable to be dismissed in recent years as flawed by blatant Elizabethan jingoism: little more than an assertively patriotic pageant in which a charismatic but predatory sovereign, after self-righteously justifying his thirst for battle with arguments of dubious legality, proceeds to lead an ill-equipped band of humble soldiers into danger on a totally ruthless quest

Introduction

for territorial aggrandizement and personal glory. The fact that so many of Henry's sounding phrases have become part of the hallowed rhetoric of national self-identification –

> Cry, 'God for Harry, England, and Saint George!'
>
> We few, we happy few, we band of brothers

– has not helped to endear the work to those who reject what they see as a piece of xenophobia. The play is often dismissed as containing nothing of relevance to our own epoch, as reversing Ben Jonson's dictum on his beloved Shakespeare so that it reads:

> He was not for all time, but of an age!

That the reputedly humanitarian Swan of Avon could present this particular monarch so apparently uncritically that he seems meant to serve posterity as an example of Christian kingship is seen as offering further support for Edward Bond's unsentimentalized portrait of the Bard in *Bingo*, where Shakespeare's personal sense of probity is demonstrated to be every bit as corrupt as that of Jacobean society in general.

Even Lord Olivier's cinematic air of conviction has recently been shown to be somewhat less than instinctive: in his autobiography, *Confessions of an Actor*, he reveals how, called upon to play Henry at the Old Vic in 1937, he found the heroic and declamatory aspects of his role so distasteful that he took the problem to the late Ralph Richardson. Richardson's response was blandly benign: yes, he recognized that on the face of it Henry appeared to be a 'boring old scout-master', but since Shakespeare had created him, he stood for 'the exaltation of all scout-masters. He's the cold-bath kind, and you have to glory in it.' It seems to have been only this advice, coupled with Charles Laughton's reverential tribute, 'You're *England*!', that helped the player to conquer his intuitive dislike of the role. (It was, presumably, an easier matter for Olivier to relish the part when making the screen version in 1943–4, with Britain heavily engaged in a major combat of worldwide dimensions.)

Certainly, the character both of the historical Henry and of Shakespeare's dramatic treatment of him is enigmatic, and one of our tasks must be to attempt to establish what the playwright found of intrinsic interest in the figure of the king. Some claim that the dramatist was merely succumbing to 'box-office pressure' in composing a finale to a sequence which began with *Richard II* and *Henry IV*, and that Henry as a personality interested him not at all. By this token, he was content to depict him as the essence of virtue and leave it at that. Yet, if there were nothing more to Henry than the idealized Baden-Powell figure of Ralph

Masterstudies: Henry V

Richardson, there would be little need for this book. Few plays of significance assume an unequivocal attitude towards human personality, and it seems unlikely that even a great national hero such as Henry would have failed to inspire at least a measure of critical scrutiny from an Elizabethan author as astute and as alive to ironies and ambiguities as Shakespeare, who rarely takes human beings at face-value.

Not that we should give our exclusive attention to 'character'. The general importance which the Elizabethans and their seventeenth-century successors attached to the whole subject which we think of as history has a significant place in determining our response. To people of that period, the past acted as a guide-book to the present: from a study of the prior conduct and fortunes of their human predecessors, whose deeds were variously set forth in chronicle form, men and women believed that salutary lessons could be learnt, valuable precedents established, ghastly mistakes avoided, previous examples emulated and terrible warnings heeded, all of which would have a favourable effect on the successful solution of contemporary dilemmas. Where we are conditioned to look on kings and queens as having feelings and personalities substantially like our own, Shakespeare's contemporaries viewed them, both in historical perspective and as people, as beings whose qualities and abilities had a powerfully symbolic significance for those over whom they reigned, which gave their characters more than mere psychological interest. Hence, aside from Henry's intrinsically individual features, we must also learn to regard him as fulfilling for the Elizabethans a representative function as a national icon, as a figure embodying certain monarchical traits made manifest in medieval English history, which could plausibly be expected to serve as an inspiration to those reading his deeds in the pages of the chroniclers or witnessing their manifestation on the public stages of London during the latter part of 1599. Shakespeare's age was still able to see beyond a mortal embodiment of royalty to contemplate the mystic significance of the office he or she performed.

This study takes its starting-point from the not unreasonable assumption that in writing *Henry V* Shakespeare brought alive and made meaningful for his contemporaries the historical deeds and the personality of a man who for them represented the nation's most respected medieval king. All creative writers who turn to history for inspiration have to accept that this procedure will impose certain limitations on the free and unrestrained exercise of their imaginations, and Shakespeare, in common with many authors of his time, had to come to terms with the problems inherent in utilizing the stuff of history as the basis for literature. Necessarily, therefore, some space will be given to the actual historical figure of Henry himself, and to the manner in which over the

Introduction

centuries chroniclers and historians assessed his character and achievements; we shall take less notice of modern estimations of his true calibre than of those evaluations which most influenced Shakespeare as he developed his portrait of this intriguing, if slightly daunting, figure. To set *Henry V* in its Elizabethan context will of course involve examining Shakespeare's own contribution to the impression absorbed by his contemporaries, since the young Henry plays a leading role in both parts of *Henry IV*, completed not long before the composition of their sequel. One question we shall need to pose is whether *Henry V* is a self-contained play or not, or whether Shakespeare worked on the assumption that his audiences for the later piece were already familiar with Henry and other characters as they appear in the two *Henry IV* plays. These earlier appearances may be assumed to colour or balance out the impression which we take away from *Henry V* itself.

There is another matter to be considered: Shakespeare was not the only Elizabethan playwright to employ Henry as a hero of a historical chronicle play. One of his chief debts was undoubtedly to an anonymous piece first staged some years before, published in 1598 as *The Famous Victories of Henry the fifth*. This somewhat crude and uncouth play (which for us exists only in a mutilated text) was the source for a number of scenes and incidents in both parts of *Henry IV* and in *Henry V*. Moreover, in its depiction of Henry both as prince and king, the earlier play created certain expectations in the minds of Elizabethan playgoers which not even Shakespeare saw fit to ignore or to counteract. (The same probably applies to his approach to *Hamlet*.) Hence, a number of factors prevented Shakespeare from exercising totally independent control over his dramatic creation: the age's expectations of history as an admonitory or exemplary form; the chroniclers' estimation of the monarchy and its perception by the Elizabethan public at large; the example provided by at least one previous presentation of the king on stage; and Shakespeare's own earlier treatment of Henry V before his ascent to the throne.

Lastly, before settling to a close and detailed analysis of the play text itself, we need to consider briefly the question of Shakespeare's handling of war, since military conflict obviously plays a notable part in *Henry V*, and is the focal point of a good deal of the action. It is worth remembering that throughout almost the whole of Shakespeare's working life, England was at war with somebody somewhere, in the sense that her armed forces were engaged in combat with a foreign power, whether there had been a formal declaration of hostilities or not. There are even those commentators who feel that some of the so-called 'missing years' in Shakespeare's life (in the second half of the 1580s) were spent in the

Masterstudies: Henry V

army, which might account for his apparent knowledge of the talking-points and technicalities of contemporary warfare. This must be speculative – after all, textbooks on tactics and weaponry were available to non-combatants – but whatever the truth, we should certainly be wary of endowing Shakespeare with our own late twentieth-century sensibilities when we come to inspect the attitudes to war which inform his plays. It would be remarkable if a sixteenth-century Englishman, brought up in the conventions of an age so different from ours, had anticipated the reactions and opinions of those born some four hundred years later. Jonson's famous tribute (reversed in a previous paragraph) may contain more truth than falsehood, and the playwright's reputed universality may be a major factor in his perennial appeal, but the disappointment expressed by some critics, that this great literary genius did not share their own liberal and humanitarian ideals, is misplaced. Great authors are not great by virtue of the acceptability of their choice of subject-matter or of their ethical or political viewpoints to succeeding generations.

Then the time will be ripe for examining the text of *Henry V* in detail. After a short introduction to the play's textual history, we shall proceed to consider the principal elements of *Henry V*, examining its structure, the characteristic qualities of its language and the forms which that takes, its characterization and the nature of its themes, as separable entities, although every reader or playgoer will readily realize that one can no more treat these vital aspects of a work of literature as if they were unrelated, than one can extract from a beautifully baked cake the eggs, fat, flour, sugar, and fruit which contributed to the perfection of the whole. But it is hoped that by treating the ingredients in this way, a gradually deepening appreciation of the play as a whole will be effected.

In the course of these discussions of the play – of its structure, language, characterization and themes – we shall of course need to seek assistance from the play's critics from time to time. They will not be easy to cold-shoulder completely during the earlier sections of the book, but it may be advisable to defer appealing to too many conflicting judgements and opinions until we ourselves have sifted the evidence, reached some decisions and have formed views of our own. At that point we can most profitably subject our own independent reading of the text to the test of seeing how it stands up to the scrutiny of others who have travelled the same route before us, even if they were differently equipped for the journey. All that needs to be said now is that we should always be on our guard against formulating a hard and fast judgement on the basis of inadequate or superficial evidence. 'Keeping an open mind' should be the aim in literary criticism as in so many other human judgements. This is where those critics who have formulated their views ahead of ours can

Introduction

prove most helpful; they can remind us to be wary of accepting the literary or ethical standards of our own period as having absolute validity, or of viewing any complex work of art from an exclusive standpoint, be it politically, theologically, sociologically, sexually or aesthetically orientated. Any critics worth reading should be able to demonstrate to us just how multi-faceted a work of art is, and not merely annex it in the name of a single vested interest. If the *Henry V* of many people's analyses or memories seems to consist of nothing more than battle-scenes and fiery speeches extolling slaughter, it is important that at least one critic should remind us that some of the action takes place off the field of conflict, nowhere near the walls of some beleaguered city. Henry may exhibit tendencies which would qualify him as a first-rate scout-master, but we must also see him in other roles, as statesman, private individual, practical joker, negotiator, even (possibly least convincingly) lover, or, at any rate, wooer. The piece may appear to exalt the great ones who lead their troops into battle –

> Harry the King, Bedford and Exeter,
>
> ... Dukes of Berri and of Britaine,
> Of Brabant and of Orleans

– but it also spares a thought for the common soldiery whose function as in another celebrated British action seems to be 'but to do and die'. The play may abound in speeches conveying the glamour of warfare, but a good critic will also remind us that it also expresses in memorable terms the horror, degradation and suffering which are unleashed when nations engage in armed aggression:

> our houses and ourselves and children
> Have lost, or do not learn for want of time,
> The sciences that should become our country,
> But grow like savages – as soldiers will
> That nothing do but meditate on blood ...

However, the central sections of this study will not seek to confront the explorer with too many critical responses to the play, and perhaps as a result of keeping the professional critics in check, their true value may be perceived, that is, as collaborators with us in our task of deciding, in the light of our own tastes and experiences, what this play has to say to us rather than as suppliers of ready-made points-of-view. In this manner we can look at *Henry V* as a piece of literary and dramatic art to which we can truly claim to have responded personally and not by proxy.

After the literary analysis must come some attempt to assess the impact of the play as theatre, its first as well as its final proving-ground. A good

Masterstudies: Henry V

deal has been written in recent years to redress the injustice done to drama by former scholars and critics who seemed oblivious of the theatrical purpose and impact of plays when they came to discuss them as literature: today it is scarcely necessary to remind readers that a play when staged may prove to offer a very different experience from that play when read. Our approach will be to look at *Henry V* in the theatre from its earliest recorded performances. A reading of the play does not always take into account its effect when it is acted before an audience, whether that audience is in a theatre or watching a film or television. A Henry who repels us on the cold printed page may delight us or engage our sympathies when encountered in a stirring or moving performance from a convincing actor. Nor can we neglect in performance something that in reading we can often slide over: despite its military theme and the seriousness of its doctrinal content, this is a play which contains a number of unheroic, comic sequences (some broad, some more subtly ironic) whose contribution to the total dramatic impression is substantial. A first-class production of any play can often bring out those elements which in reading we are only too prone to underestimate or miss altogether. On the other hand, live performances can sometimes overemphasize or gloss over essential aspects of the text. Neither approach can afford to ignore the other.

The aim of the short section which concludes the book is to try and achieve a balanced view of the play, based on a synthesis of what has gone before. Discussion of *Henry V* can obviously never be brought to a definitive once-and-for-all conclusion; a work of art is a constantly changing organism, and every experience we undergo, every piece of information we acquire, if it has relevance to that work, must influence our opinion of it. Throughout our lives, we should be modifying and developing our attitude to Shakespeare's work in general, and to each individual play in particular.

History and the Elizabethans

It is because certain expectations and preconceptions lay behind the Elizabethans' attitudes to their historical past that one approach to *Henry V* has to be through the medium of history. Shakespeare's drama does not purport to be pure documentary, any more than any play of today dealing with historical events and characters would: one of the author's tasks was undoubtedly to render a period of history intelligible to his contemporaries. The playwright did not work in a social or political limbo: the age he lived in and the attitude it adopted towards its own past inevitably influenced his treatment, coloured his selection and presentation and shaped what he inherited from his sources.

It is of course impossible to assess just how much history the average man or woman in the Elizabethan street was familiar with. Without access to radio or television, or cheap but authoritative paperbacks, their horizons were in many respects more limited than ours; but we should not neglect the powerful role played by oral tradition in developing some awareness of bygone ages. Certainly there is no denying that the Elizabethans appear to have attached a great deal of significance to what the pages of history had to communicate to them; as Louis B. Wright says in his *Middle-Class Culture in Elizabethan England*, 'The Elizabethan citizen shared the belief of his learned and courtly contemporaries that the reading of history was an exercise second only to the study of Holy Writ in its power to induce good morality and shape the individual into a worthy member of society.'

This statement can be most readily illustrated by considering the significant number of chronicle or history plays which make their appearance in England during the last quarter of the sixteenth century, a period when the country was busily cultivating a sense of patriotic identity within a European community whose rival kingdoms were all largely promulgating similarly vigorous brands of assertive nationalism. Although many plays of an earlier vintage may have failed to survive, there does seem to have been an upsurge in production between the year of the Spanish Armada in 1588 and the turn of the century. A chronological list in Irving Ribner's survey, *The English History Play in the Age of Shakespeare*, cites some thirty extant chronicle plays from roughly these years, testament to the popularity of the form. Of course, there are many reasons to account for the attraction of the history play at this time: its

Masterstudies: Henry V

capacity to exploit as well as encourage a sense of increasing national solidarity in the face of a Catholic foe; the opportunities it offered aspiring, pioneering playwrights for striking or sensational stage-effects, most notably in terms of battle-scenes; the manner in which its contents could often satisfy the public's desire to be privy to the deliberations and decisions of kings, princes and governors. But overriding these undoubtedly appealing features seems to have been the belief that past history offered both statesmen and subjects a handy sourcebook of telling examples on which to base both political and personal decisions and judgements, and from which sound conclusions might be reliably drawn regarding individual conduct and national policy.

This tradition had been established early in the sixteenth century with such pieces as John Bale's prototype history play, *King Johan*, with its strong anti-Catholic flavour, and Sackville and Norton's *Gorboduc*, with its covert advice that Queen Elizabeth should take a husband for the future good of her realm. But the importance the Elizabethans attached to historical precedent may be most strikingly illustrated from a little-known but excellent historical drama of *c.* 1592, generally referred to as *Woodstock*, but actually entitled *The Tragedy of Thomas of Woodstock* (most readily accessible in W. A. Armstrong's World's Classics collection, *Elizabethan History Plays*). The piece, which unfortunately lacks a few final pages, tells the story of the reign of Richard II up to the point at which Shakespeare's dramatic treatment of that controversial sovereign begins and, indeed, without some knowledge of the events contained in it – particularly the presentation of Richard's abuse of power and his connivance at the murder of his uncle Thomas of Woodstock, Lord Protector of England – some of the earlier portion of Shakespeare's text is difficult to follow.

In Act II, Scene 1 of *Woodstock*, Richard comes upon one of his companions, Bushy, reading from the historical accounts of the deeds of the king's illustrious ancestors:

> KING
> How now, what readst thou, Bushy?
> BUSHY
> The monuments of English Chronicles,
> Containing acts and memorable deeds
> Of all your famous predecessor kings.
> KING
> What findst thou of them?
> BUSHY
> Examples strange and wonderful, my lord,
> The end of treason even in mighty persons:

> For here 'tis said your royal grandfather,
> Took the Protector then, proud Mortimer,
> And on a gallows fifty foot in height
> He hung him for his pride and treachery.
>
> KING
> Why should our proud Protector then presume
> And we not punish him, whose treason's viler far
> Than ever was rebellious Mortimer?
> Prithee read on: examples such as these
> Will bring us to our kingly grandsire's spirit.
> What's next?
>
> BUSHY
> The battle full of dread and doubtful fear
> Was fought between your father and the French.
>
> KING
> Read on, we'll hear it.
>
> [Bushy reads an account of the Black Prince's feats at the Battle of Poitiers.]
>
> KING
> A victory most strange and admirable.
> Never was conquest got with such great odds.
> O princely Edward, had thy son such hap,
> Such fortune and success to follow him,
> His daring uncles and rebellious peers
> Durst not control and govern as they do.
> But these bright shining trophies shall awake me,
> And as we are his body's counterfeit,
> So will we be the image of his mind,
> And die but we'll attain his virtuous deeds.

Richard II is thus depicted turning to historical precedent like any good Elizabethan to supply him with the necessary role-models for executing his intended plans.

But the events and personalities of history can of course be interpreted in different ways, to suit almost any political, moral or social position or affiliation. To take one instance, for the anonymous author of *Woodstock*, the king's uncle exemplifies seagreen incorruptibility and ardent love of one's native land, whereas Richard II is presented as a degenerate and a treacherous tyrant who seeks to exploit the kingdom for his own pecuniary advantage. On the other hand, to Jean Froissart, the great French chronicler and contemporary of Richard, and indeed to most modern historians, Woodstock brought disaster on himself through overbearing acts of provocation, cruelty and rebellion, and richly deserved his death, however violent. This notion finds an echo in the works of the celebrated Elizabethan historian, Raphael Holinshed, who in the 1587 edition of his *Chronicles of England, Scotland and Ireland*

Masterstudies: Henry V

describes the duke as 'fierce of nature, hastie, wilfull and given more to war than to peace', and characterizes Richard II as 'a prince the most unthankfully used of his subjects of anyone of whom ye shall lightly read'. Like us, Elizabethan readers (and of course Elizabethan writers) were accustomed to receive their historical information coloured by those imparting it.

As a result, the dominant thought-patterns which underlie the Elizabethan interpretation of events in English history must be regarded as far less uniform than was once considered to be the case. Those eminent scholars who pioneered the exploration of the English chronicle-play and Shakespeare's radical development of the form were over-inclined to suggest that all Tudor historians spoke with one voice, not merely on such topical issues as law and order, obedience to authority and the vital importance of the notion of hierarchy, but on the moral and political significance of the principal figures and the key incidents of the recent past. In particular, it was assumed that in composing his histories Shakespeare was following the moralistic treatment of the kings of England between Richard II and Richard III. This treatment was embodied by propagandists in the so-called 'Tudor Myth' of history, which was dedicated to the proposition that Henry VII's accession to the English throne in 1485 lifted a divine curse which had struck the country in 1399, when Richard II was unlawfully deposed by Henry Bolingbroke, later Henry IV. But as Robert Ornstein in *A Kingdom for a Stage* (1972) pointed out, there was not merely diversity of opinion among sixteenth-century writers regarding the relative merits of Richard and Bolingbroke, but also a wide range of conclusions as to the precise lessons that history in general could be presumed to teach. Ornstein went on to demonstrate how unlikely it was that Shakespeare would be willing to act as a semi-official apologist for Elizabethan orthodoxies, even if one could firmly establish what precisely those orthodoxies were: 'If we grant that there was in Shakespeare's England a community of shared values and beliefs which scholarship can cautiously describe, we must grant too that a wide range of individual and group attitudes must have existed in his society, which knew more than its share of religious and political turmoil and social and economic change.' Even more recently, Jonathan Dollimore has argued in *Radical Tragedy* that the work of Shakespeare and his contemporaries was far more subversive, socially, politically and ideologically, than is usually accepted: it is clear that we generalize about 'Elizabethan attitudes', and Shakespeare's response to them, at our peril.

However, it is perhaps safe to assert that, in the main, Elizabethan historians tended to confine their freedom of interpretation to certain

History and the Elizabethans

identifiable areas, and that there was probably a greater consensus of opinion among them concerning the principal patterns that could be detected in historical events than there might be among a comparable body of experts today. While individual chroniclers might differ as to the degree of emphasis to be placed on certain central events or idiosyncratic traits of personality, in general they were disinclined to advance exclusive or unorthodox opinions when it came to assessing the overall import of the reign of an individual monarch as far as it affected the nation as a whole. No Tudor historian seems to have set out to idolize the allegedly crookbacked figure of Richard III, or expressed satisfaction at the disastrous effects of the Wars of the Roses; no one seems less than enthusiastic about what Edward Hall refers to as the 'victorious actes of kyng Henry the V'. Thus, in dealing with the reigns of Richard II, Henrys IV, V and VI, and Richard III, Shakespeare could scarcely fail to be aware of a certain sense of agreement among those historians who were his contemporaries, which is certainly not to suggest for one moment that he simply followed their opinions in a slavish fashion. The independence of Shakespeare's intellect and artistic imagination is nowhere more apparent than in his handling of the matter of English history, yet even he could not ignore established opinion entirely. Thus a few observations concerning 'shared values and beliefs' may be pertinent, provided that we advance them with the degree of cautiousness advocated by Professor Ornstein.

Certainly we must begin by discarding the notion promulgated by E. M. W. Tillyard at the time of Olivier's film, and subsequently supported by others, that Shakespeare's histories endorse the officially sanctioned interpretation of fifteenth-century English history. The Tudors may have seen themselves (or been persuaded to see themselves) as providentially elected to heal the wounds of the Wars of the Roses and restore the country to God's gracious favour, but the very existence of an official viewpoint on any subject is more likely to promote scepticism or opposition than acquiescence, particularly among creative artists (in their art, if not their lives). It can never be stressed enough that Shakespeare was a dramatist and as such could advance in the course of one scene half-a-dozen contradictory opinions in succession and never be detected as identifying with any one of them. For example, the suggestion that in Canterbury's speech in *Henry V* (where he employs the image of the honey-bee to parallel the workings of an ideal community), we hear Shakespeare's voice commending the way heaven divides

> The state of man in divers functions,
> Setting endeavour in continual motion;

Masterstudies: Henry V

> To which is fixed as an aim or butt
> Obedience...
>
> (I. 2. 184–7)

ignores the nature of drama. Are speeches supportive of the status quo any more likely to embody Shakespeare's own position than those which express rebellious or even anarchic sentiments? Can we ever know what Shakespeare's opinions were on any subject, outside the sonnets? As Margaret Cavendish, Duchess of Newcastle, wrote in 1664: '... so Well he hath Express'd in his Playes all Sorts of Persons, as one would think he had been Transformed into every one of those Persons he hath Described...'

On the other hand, if Shakespeare is not to be regarded as a topical purveyor of received ideas concerning the Tudor body politic, it is also true that we cannot maintain that he was immune to or untouched by them, in so far as they appear to have been widely promulgated. Tacit acknowledgement of the importance of hierarchy – 'knowing one's place' – in society, of the wickedness of disobedience towards one's familial or social superiors, of the sinfulness of rebellion and private vengeance, of respect for authority, seems to have been constantly demanded of the restless and volatile Tudor citizens, and indoctrinated by means of some fairly thorough methods of propaganda, which included the regular and compulsory reading of the famous *Homilies* or authorized sermons in the churches of Shakespeare's youth. Elizabethans were being ceaselessly urged, from the pulpit, by tracts, in government pronouncements, to support a system which, they were taught to believe, would ensure them of God's approval and the government's good will. The alternative, they were told, was chaos.

Nor should we, conditioned by our late twentieth-century outlook, automatically assume that all Elizabethan citizens paid lip-service only to such a view, or that successive governments were bluffing when they urged the importance of harmony and conformity in the state. As we shall see in a later section, 'Shakespeare and War', Elizabethan England was vulnerable both to attack from without and anarchy within; the queen was far from secure on her throne, and even if she survived into maturity, there was still the vexed question of the succession. Hence the frequent calls that Elizabeth should marry and beget an heir to ensure the future of the realm. During the sixteenth century alien powers were constantly watching for an opportunity to strike at England's foundations, and any kind of civil unrest, if it got out of hand, might provide the perfect opportunity to mischief-makers.

History and the Elizabethans

Thus it was that the Elizabethans in their reading of history tended to value instances of strong, positive leadership from the top, to look unfavourably on rebellion as weakening the fabric of society and to deplore those displays of human folly which put the nation's safety or prosperity at risk. Their admiration appears to have been unfailingly sought for authoritative monarchs such as Edward I or Henry V, who were indisputedly in command of their kingdom, in contrast to men like Edward II, Richard II or Henry VI who, whatever their personal merits as individuals, lacked the qualities of temperament or physique which would have permitted them to impose their will on their recalcitrant subjects or take the lead in unfavourable circumstances. The Elizabethans were not sentimental in such matters: kings and queens not only had to rule, but be seen to rule.

Similarly, there seems to have been a distinct lack of general sympathy with those who sought to question or overthrow the established government; clearly all rebels and insurgents were not beyond the pale, or the various revolutionary factions that made their mark on successive Tudor governments would never have stood any chance of achieving their aims. But dissent was not generally admired. This is not to suggest that the English in the sixteenth century were depressingly conformist or orthodox in their attitudes or behaviour – subversive restlessness of a mild type, one suspects, was always current – but in the main they appear to have been prepared to accept the view embodied in the adage 'Better the devil you know than the devil you don't'; the fate of every attempt to supplant various generations of Tudors on the English throne makes this clear.

Finally, in their verdicts on such monarchs as Edward II and Richard II, the Elizabethans expressed their distaste for rulers who abused the privileges of birth or talent, who gave priority to the gratification of their personal tastes and needs over the wellbeing of their realm. In few cases was it believed that those who opposed such sovereigns were disinterested parties. But the Elizabethans do appear to have had some basic belief in what might have been called 'the good of the country as a whole', and their view of England's past history was governed in many respects by this. This obviously permitted a wide range of arguments to be deployed for or against some central historical event, most notably perhaps the deposition of the legitimate monarch, Richard II, by his cousin Henry Bolingbroke, in 1399. Henry was clearly the more efficient ruler, but establishing whether *his* action was for 'the good of the country as a whole' occupied many hours of debate and much expenditure of ink and paper. For Shakespeare the dramatist (whatever he thought as an individual citizen) it was the sort of division of opinion that provided him with some of his finest opportunities as a playwright. It will be the business of this book to discover whether or not the historical Henry V offered the same dialectical opportunities.

The Man and the Myth

King Henry V of England was born at Monmouth Castle in South Wales on 16 September 1387, and died, probably of dysentery, at Vincennes Castle south-east of Paris on 31 August 1422, a few weeks short of his thirty-fifth birthday. He was the eldest son of Henry Bolingbroke, Duke of Hereford, and his wife Mary de Bohun who was at the most sixteen when the first of her six children was born. (She died in childbirth in July 1394, and both her husband and eldest son seem to have revered her memory.) The stages by which Bolingbroke, as heir to his father, John of Gaunt's, dukedom of Lancaster, backed into the limelight as a claimant to the throne of his cousin Richard II are too complex to rehearse here, but his title to the crown was a tenuous one, not least because the descendants of Lionel, Duke of Clarence, second son of Edward III and brother to both the Black Prince and John of Gaunt, had a prior claim. Banished from England by Richard in October 1398, Bolingbroke returned the following summer ostensibly to claim the Lancastrian heritage Richard had denied him in February on the death of his father, but actually to force the lawful king into abdication, and to succeed him as Henry IV in October 1399.

At the time of Bolingbroke's coup, the future Henry V was barely twelve years old, a handsome, well-tutored, cultivated boy, fond of music and reading, and by a not uncommon irony of the period, probably better acquainted with the deposed Richard than with his own father. The ex-king had made much of his cousin's son, even during the months of his father's exile, and when Bolingbroke reappeared in England, the boy doubtless found his loyalties divided between a royal patron who had recently knighted him on an ill-fated campaign in Ireland, and a parental rebel whose bid for the crown now had profound implications for his heir. Richard's general unpopularity and his own bold ruthlessness favoured Bolingbroke, and before 1399 was out Henry of Monmouth had rapidly become Duke of Cornwall, Earl of Chester, Duke of both Aquitaine and Lancaster, and Prince of Wales. An almost-successful plot against the lives of the new king and his sons, intended for Twelfth Night 1400, hastened the death of Richard at Pontefract Castle; whether murder or maltreatment was the precise cause, it is likely that Henry IV had knowledge of its instigation.

Richard's untimely death cast a long shadow over the reign of his

Masterstudies: Henry V

successor, and as we have already noted, some claimed that it was the culmination of a crime of such impiety that the country was to languish under a heavenly sentence of almost ninety years' misfortune before the Tudors arrived to lift the curse. Certainly the earlier portion of Bolingbroke's relatively short reign was devoted to strenuous efforts to consolidate and defend his precarious position, and as his eldest son, Prince Henry was expected to play a full role in establishing the authority of the new regime. But it was not an easy task: Bolingbroke for all his ambition did not have a strong physical constitution, and Henry for all his martial prowess was still in his teens.

However, he had already experienced stirring events and now, under fresh pressures, he necessarily matured rapidly. Seemingly possessed of tremendous mental and physical resources, accompanied by an abundance of charisma, Henry was to spend his formative years developing into a seasoned military campaigner within his own principality of Wales. The Welsh, who had been among Richard II's most loyal supporters, were more than willing to grapple with the traditional enemy, England, and an excellent reason for doing so seemed to arise with a land dispute between one of the Marcher lords, Reginald Grey of Ruthin, and an affluent and cultured Welsh magnate, Owain Glyndŵr. In September 1400 Prince Henry became a junior member of the first of several abortive English expeditions to bring the recalcitrant Welsh to heel, and bad faith on both sides meant that before long an essentially local skirmish had escalated into full-scale rebellion against both the army of occupation and the English living across Offa's Dyke.

For a time, the Welsh leader carried all before him and the royal forces could only engage in savage reprisals. Possibly the most dangerous period for Henry IV came in 1403, when the ever-ambitious Percy family – formerly supporters of Bolingbroke in his quest to recover his ducal rights – made an alliance with the Scottish Earl of Douglas, with the intention of replacing Bolingbroke on the throne with the Earl of March, nephew to Sir Edmund Mortimer, Glyndŵr's son-in-law. By this time Prince Henry was in full command on the Marches, his former mentor, Harry Percy (nicknamed Hotspur), son of the wily Earl of Northumberland, having resigned his commission in Wales and retired north to nurture his sense of grievance at the usurper's alleged lack of gratitude. Northumberland's faction under Hotspur and his uncle, Thomas, Earl of Worcester, and the Scots under Douglas marched south in the hope of linking up with Glyndŵr, but on 21 July 1403 at the Battle of Shrewsbury the combined troops of the king and his eldest son inflicted a heavy defeat on them, with the prince, not yet sixteen, exhibiting not only considerable military skill but personal courage after sustaining an

The Man and the Myth

arrow-wound to the face. Hotspur was killed, his uncle taken prisoner and beheaded, and the alliance with Glyndŵr aborted.

Notwithstanding the loss of such powerful allies, the Welsh insurgents continued as a thorn in Bolingbroke's flesh, harrying castles in both North and South Wales: in 1404 Glyndŵr signed a treaty which guaranteed French military assistance. A year later, an indenture between Northumberland, Mortimer and the Welsh leader partitioned England and Wales between the allies, who scented victory: uprisings at home and foreign invasions followed in its wake, and it was not until the French had lost interest, several distinguished conspirators had been removed and both Mortimer and Northumberland had been killed that the tide began to turn in Bolingbroke's favour. Prince Henry campaigned incessantly and often ruthlessly to recover control of his principality, acquiring a superb knowledge of warfare in the process, and proving himself a loyal supporter of his father's interests throughout a period when his future seemed precarious. Although guerrilla warfare dragged on in Wales for some time, after about 1407 it no longer constituted a threat to Henry IV's survival on the English throne.

The latter part of his reign, however, saw father and son estranged for long periods; the reasons are not difficult to guess. Perhaps the seeds of dissension were sown with the prince's initial loyalty to Richard II; perhaps he was over-eager to demonstrate his own abilities to a monarch sometimes rendered incapable from ill-health and regarded as old before his time. Yet Bolingbroke had no intention of abrogating his responsibilities even to a confident and accomplished Heir Apparent whom he only suffered to deputize for him on occasions when sickness dictated it. Given that the prince was sometimes permitted to exercise authority and sometimes restrained from doing so, family friction was almost inevitable. Neither the king nor his son lacked for influential allies, so that faction and intrigue darkened the later years of the relationship. However, although there is no doubt that sovereign and crown prince were often alienated, there is little substance in the popular myth ascribing Henry IV's disaffection to the riotous excesses of his son's salad days.

Yet, equally, there is no reason to disbelieve in the prince's enthusiastic pursuit of heady sensual pleasures: such youthful hedonism represents the soldier home on leave or the other face of the diligent, dedicated politician, much involved with tedious details of national finance or foreign relations, and with maintaining the rule of law. Without question, like almost every young healthy male of his class and era, Henry sowed his wild oats, but it also seems clear that at his father's death, which occurred on 20 March 1413, his successor solemnly pledged himself

Masterstudies: Henry V

within the walls of Westminster Abbey to conduct himself with becoming gravity and even a degree of piety, the novelty of which was much remarked upon (and approved of) by his contemporaries. Whatever his faults, Henry V must be said to have treated his royal office with commendable seriousness.

His reign lasted for almost nine and a half years, and although one may have reservations regarding the legacy he bequeathed to his infant son – and no one can be blamed for dying with his life's work incomplete – one cannot but admire Henry's determination, energy and executive abilities in making the fullest possible use of his time on the English throne. How far his cherished project of conquering France as his rightful inheritance, and then leading the combined forces of France and England on a latter-day crusade to the Holy Land, was inspired by religious devotion rather than territorial acquisitiveness or diversionary tactics can never be ascertained, but he clearly saw in a France weakened by civil strife a plum ripe for picking, as well as the opportunity for uniting the English aristocracy behind the crown in a popular foray on to hallowed battleground. His refusal to be bought off by offers to concede to him large tracts of land along with the hand of the king's daughter clutching a handsome dowry suggests either greediness or a conviction as to the justification of his claim to rule over the whole of France. French resistance to what they viewed as presumption increased the sense of self-righteous indignation and swelled the coffers of the proposed expedition, although a conspiracy to overthrow Henry – revealed just before the invasion force left Southampton – demonstrated that support for the war was not universal. (Once again the luckless Earl of March was the favoured substitute had the nobles' plot succeeded in its aim: on this occasion the earl saved his own neck by sacrificing his sponsors'.)

Henry's intrusion into Europe in 1415 offers one further instance of near-disaster miraculously converted into military triumph. Crossing the Channel with no more than 10,000 men, Henry promptly set about besieging Harfleur at the mouth of the Seine, a town renowned for its strong defences. The siege lasted only five weeks, but it was long enough for the invading army to become riddled with dysentery and fever: probably some 2,000 soldiers died, while as many as 5,000 may have had to be sent back to England. Since Harfleur was freely surrendered, the king did not sack it as he had threatened, but he took its leading citizens prisoner and evicted many of its inhabitants, albeit with their belongings intact. The capture of Harfleur had cost his army dear, and many of his advisers now urged him to return to England before winter's ravages reduced his decrepit invasion force still more drastically.

But Henry was not to be deterred: aware that he could scarcely return

The Man and the Myth

home with so little to show for his pains and bolstered by what seems to have been immeasurable faith both in himself and his Maker, he resolved to march east to take ship for England from Calais, then an English possession, some two hundred miles away, despite reports that the French were amassing a huge force at Rouen, only fifty miles from Harfleur. The journey proved wearisome and hazardous, and it required a wide detour to find a suitable place for the English troops to cross the River Somme safe from the French force, who by now were harrying and menacing their opponents. After some hesitation and parleying, the French leaders blocked the Calais road close to the village of Agincourt, and challenged the King of England to a pitched battle. He attempted to make terms at this point – whether in all sincerity or as a ruse to persuade his opponents that his force was weaker than it was we can never know – and then set about preparing his men for the seemingly unequal conflict which was to take place the following morning.

The rest is history. The French army was superior in numbers, but poorly led, divided in its allegiances and badly disciplined; the English had a sole commander, were brilliantly led and had been well trained. After a night of torrential rain, the ground between the armies was waterlogged, which hampered the heavily armoured French spearmen, who were the mainstay of their army, and made them easy targets for the deadly accuracy of the English longbowmen. The cavalry on the French flanks were rapidly rendered ineffective, and in the ensuing mêlée those of their compatriots who were on foot were butchered in their hundreds, one wave after another being reduced to groaning heaps. Henry threw himself unsparingly into the thick of the fighting, performing valiant deeds and taking hard knocks, the only seeming blemish on his chivalrous reputation the order to slaughter all prisoners except those likely to yield a valuable ransom, the excuse being that he feared a counter-attack from the cavalry on a force still vulnerable, even in the moment of their victory. The astonishing discrepancy between the heavy French casualty figures and those of their opponents strengthened Henry's ardent conviction that the defeat of England's traditional foe should be credited to the favour of God and not to her own prowess in arms.

Great were the rejoicings in Calais when Henry arrived there four days after the battle, and even more lavish was the welcome in London when the victorious sovereign entered his capital on 23 November 1415. Whether his famous victory of 25 October at Agincourt secured any lasting benefits for the realm must be doubted, but at least it ensured that Henry's personal authority was never questioned again. Moreover, on the Continent he was now a force to be reckoned with: the Pope praised his strength in warfare, the Holy Roman Emperor Sigismund

Masterstudies: Henry V

treated him as an equal and ultimately signed a treaty with him, which left Henry free to continue his campaign to recover France, whose defenders, although still weakened by internecine rivalries, were capable of mounting daunting counter-attacks on the foreign invader occupying the Harfleur region.

Henry prepared carefully for his second cross-Channel sortie, securing both financial and military support before embarking; on 31 July 1417 a formidable army of horse and foot crossed from Southampton to France to begin the conquest of Normandy. This took the form of a long drawn-out process of successively besieging the major fortified towns and castles in turn: Caen was sacked, Falaise surrendered and by the end of July 1418 Rouen itself was under siege. Henry's remorseless insistence on discipline and detail now proved decisive, as the city was gradually starved into submission during the autumn and winter months by a merciless foe who refused 12,000 non-combatants – expelled from the beleaguered town – permission to pass through the English lines to safety, leaving many to perish from exposure and malnutrition. Eventually on 19 January 1419 Rouen capitulated.

Henry had also kept up the pressure on the diplomatic front, and the capture of Rouen strengthened his hand considerably; on the other hand, under threat from a common foe, the French were inclined to forget their differences and unite, and Henry's success story might have been very different had it not been for the treachery of the dauphin's faction, who murdered the Duke of Burgundy during diplomatic negotiations and played right into the hands of the English king. An alliance with the Burgundians guaranteed Henry the French crown on the death of Charles VI and the hand of the French princess, in exchange for his assistance in avenging the death of the murdered duke. On 21 May 1420 these provisions were ratified by the Treaty of Troyes, and the king and Katherine were married twelve days later.

But Henry's martial aspirations left him little time for matrimony: a single day sufficed for a honeymoon, and he then returned to the campaign; the pattern of siege and advance was repeated with increasing ruthlessness and apparent brutality on the king's part. Early in 1421 he felt secure enough in his new possessions to return home for five months, receiving adulation and renewed financial backing, although the peremptory demands for the latter seemingly tempered the unanimity of the former. But the task of consolidating his tenuous hold over France called him back to attack a number of strongholds held by the dauphin's supporters in the vicinity of Paris. It was probably while besieging the fortress of Meaux during the winter of 1421–2 that Henry contracted the debilitating illness which eventually killed him. The capitulation of

The Man and the Myth

Meaux in May 1422 was his last great military success; eager to assist the Burgundians to relieve the siege at Cosne, he struggled to Vincennes, where he died at the end of August, having arranged his affairs and those of his country with that cool efficiency so typical of him.

Undoubtedly much of the glamour attached to Henry's name in subsequent decades derived from the contrast it offered to the bitter gloom of ensuing events. The loss of all that had been achieved in France; the domestic traumas of the reign of Henry VI, culminating in the wasteful viciousness of the Wars of the Roses; these things helped to give to the brief reign of Henry V that aura of prosperous wellbeing sometimes attributed to the Edwardian 'garden-party' era which preceded the agonies of World War I. It is an undeniable fact that few modern historians have felt able to give unqualified approval to either Henry's character or achievements: while admiring his self-discipline, his personal bravery, his capacity for planning on a large scale as well as his attention to detail and his military and diplomatic flair, they have questioned his judgement as a national leader, and in particular the long-term wisdom of his foreign policy. Conceding that we cannot judge his conduct in battle by the ethical standards of today – and even today it is manifestly plain that warfare and deprivation brutalize us all – it is still possible to see in him the humourless fanatic obsessed by what he clearly believed to be the divinely sanctioned righteousness of a mission to reclaim territories he firmly believed to be his own: territories which were being withheld from him by men guilty not only of treason but of disobedience to the will of God. Notwithstanding Henry's religious convictions, it would be easier to accept this ruthless pursuit of his aims were they not tarnished on occasion with what sounds suspiciously like personal vindictiveness.

Yet it is obviously inappropriate to dwell too long on what twentieth-century historians with all the advantages of hindsight have written about Henry's true qualities; he was what his breeding, his training and his age made him, and it is to his credit that there were also positive aspects to his contradictory personality. Energy, ability and a passion for discipline and justice were at least as pronounced in him as priggishness, inflexibility and an insistence that he alone was in the right. He had taste and he had drive; if we are disinclined to accept the valuation his own age placed upon him, let us remember that kings (and queens) did not come ready sanitized and gift-wrapped in the fifteenth century.

More central to our present purpose is to gain some insight into the image of Henry which successive generations of fifteenth- and sixteenth-century chroniclers transmitted to William Shakespeare. The tradition of the Christian warrior-king evolved rapidly in the years immediately

Masterstudies: Henry V

following Henry's death in 1422, despite the swift realization that his policies had committed the country to responsibilities it could not handle. Even during the king's lifetime a work such as the anonymous *Gesta Henrici Quinti* sought to drum up support for the second French expedition in 1417 by justifying the tactics of a devout Christian prince favoured by divine providence, and publicizing Henry's forbearance and magnanimity in the face of French duplicity and provocation. It even presents Henry as a peacemaker seeking to end hostilities between England and France by urging the French to relinquish lands being wilfully withheld from their rightful lord. In this way, Henry's deeds at Harfleur, *en route* to Agincourt, and at the battle itself are not only glorified but sanctified by one who witnessed them for himself.

However, there is no evidence to suggest that the *Gesta* was widely known among its author's contemporaries; more familiar was Thomas Elmham's *Liber Metricus de Henrico Quinto*, which drew on the *Gesta* and was in its turn the source of much that appeared in other chronicles of the period. In most of them we find Henry similarly treated as a God-guided and godly hero, anxiously seeking to right a dynastic wrong done to him by the French, and exhorting his troops to fight in the sure knowledge that they are God's chosen instrument to punish the enemy for their sins: a view which manifestly governed Henry's conduct throughout his many campaigns.

Several authors or compilers of accounts of Henry's life and accomplishments helped to inaugurate the attractive and well-known legend of his 'wild' youth and his contrition and instant conversion to piety and sobriety on his accession to his father's throne: Tito Livio, an Italian who wrote a life of Henry in about 1440, at the request of his brother, Humphrey, Duke of Gloucester, remarks that at Henry IV's death his heir

called to him a vertuous Monke of holie conversacion, to whome he confessed himselfe of all his offences, trespasses and insolencies of times past. And in all things at that time he reformed and amended his life and his manners. So after the decease of his father was never no youth nor wildnes, that might have anie place in him, but all his acts were sodenlie changed into gravitie and discretion.

The dramatic nature of the transformation is even more strikingly brought out in an English chronicle printed by William Caxton in 1480, where we read that

in his youth he had been wild and reckless, and spared nothing of his lusts and desires, but accomplished them after his liking; but as soon as he was crowned, anointed and sacred [consecrated], anon suddenly he was changed into a new man, and set all his intent to live virtuously, in maintaining of Holy Church, destroying of heretics, keeping justice, and defending of his realm and subjects.

The Man and the Myth

Also mentioned with particular favour by a number of the early chroniclers (especially those with Yorkist sympathies) is the new king's decision to re-bury the corpse of the deposed Richard II, honourably, in Westminster Abbey, some attributing his motives to a desire to clear the name of his dead father, Bolingbroke, by making some reparation for his act of usurpation. Even historians who did not support the Lancastrian view seem to have exempted Henry V from the strictures they applied to his father and to his son, Henry VI.

Another appealing tradition which originates with the earliest biographers is that of the insulting gift of tennis balls to Henry from the French dauphin; indeed, the tale is so widely attested, that it may well be regarded as having its basis in an actual happening. Elmham relays the story in the *Liber Metricus* as early as *c.* 1418, and it is significant, in light of the fact that the incident probably took place while Henry was at Kenilworth Castle in 1414, that it is a canon of Kenilworth, John Streeche, writing in about 1422, who gives us a graphic account of the occasion and Henry's response to it:

The French, in the blindness of harmful pride having no foresight, with words of gall answered foolishly to the ambassadors of the King of England, that because King Henry was young they would send him little balls to play with, and soft cushions to rest on, until what time he should grow to a man's strength. At which news the King was much troubled in spirit, yet with short, wise, and seemly words, he thus addressed those who stood about him: 'If God so wills and my life lasts, I will within a few months play such a game of ball in the Frenchmen's streets, that they shall lose their jest and gain but grief for their game. If they sleep too long upon their cushions in their chamber, perchance before they wish it I will rouse them from their slumbers by hammering on their doors at dawn.'

Admittedly, Streeche does not say that the mocking gift was actually sent, but there are several contemporary sources which do, although the donor is sometimes assumed to be the French king rather than his heir, who makes a brief appearance in an anonymous ballad on the Battle of Agincourt, sometimes attributed to John Lydgate, England's leading poet, who owed much to Henry's personal patronage:

> Grete well, he sayd, your comely kynge,
> That is bothe gentyll and small,
> A tun full of tenys balles I wyll hym send,
> For to play hym therwithall.

It is clear that throughout the fifteenth century Henry V enjoyed a unique status among those monarchs who ruled England from Richard II's time to that of Richard III, emerging with his reputation almost

Masterstudies: Henry V

totally unblemished by the disfiguring pens of historians. Only his contemporary, Adam of Usk, strikes a sour note in his *Chronicon*, compiled around 1421, when he grumbles about the high cost to the taxpayer of Henry's military exploits in France:

But woe is me! the kingdom's great ones and its treasury will be wretchedly wasted away over this affair. And without doubt, what with the insupportable taxes demanded of the people for this purpose, along with the grumblings and private curses resulting from their detestation of the unbearable burden placed on them, let us hope that my liege lord [i.e. Henry] does not end up as a partaker of the sword of God's anger!

Yet earlier even this jaundiced commentator has spoken of the king's martial valour and of 'the glory of war'!

It is difficult to say how many of these early historical accounts were known to Shakespeare: certainly very few of them were available to him in printed form, but they do of course embody a number of incidents and small touches which were passed on to posterity by means of popular myths and oral tradition, and so may have reached him by this route. Geoffrey Bullough, in his fascinating *Narrative and Dramatic Sources of Shakespeare*, volume IV, cites a number of minor details which appear in both *Henry V* and the earlier sources. Bardolph's theft of a 'pax' in Act III, Scene 6, for instance, is paralleled in the unknown chaplain's *Gesta Henrici Quinti*, where we are informed of

a certain robber, an Englishman who, in God's despite and contrary to the royal decree, had stolen and carried off from a church (perhaps thinking it was made of gold) a pyx of copper-gilt in which the Host was reserved, that pyx having been found in his sleeve. And in the next hamlet where we spent the night, by command of the king . . . and after sentence had been passed, he met his death by hanging.

Shakespeare is, however, unlikely to have known the *Gesta*; the story occurs in many accounts, in several of which Henry's remorseless concern for equity and reverence for God is the subject of favourable comment:

O Marvelous God! that of thine infinite goodnes amongest such and so manie excellent vertues hast rooted in that most vertuous Kinge so highe and perfect degree of Justice . . . undoubtedly he that shall attayne to conquests and honnour must first by th'example of this invincible conquerour conforme himself to semblable vertues.

(*The First English Life of King Henry V*, 1513)

Most of the early histories certainly contain one interesting hint that Shakespeare capitalized upon: prior to the Battle of Agincourt a knight of Henry's company (first identified as Sir Walter Hungerford) expresses a wish for the presence of a larger force. Henry's rebuke is feelingly

The Man and the Myth

conveyed in *The First English Life*, which derives in large measure from Tito Livio:

Trulie I woulde not that my companie were increased of one person more than nowe it is. Wee be, as to the regards of our enemies, but a verie smale number. But if God, of his infinit goodnes, favour our causes and right (as we surelie trust) there is none of us that may attribute this so greate a victorie to our owne power but only to the hande of God; and by that we shall the rather be provoked to give him due thanks therefore; and if peradventure for our sinns we shall be given into the hands of our enemies and to the sworde, (which God forbid) then the lesse our companie bee, the lesse domage and dishonnor shalbe to the Realme of England . . .

Subsequent retellings had ensured for Henry's speech before Agincourt almost classic status, and Shakespeare was adapting a set-piece with a venerable history when he put into the mouth of his hero the lines which begin with Henry's cheerful rejoinder to Westmorland in Act IV, Scene 3.

The principal sources of Shakespeare's information and inspiration were mainly, however, the synoptic accounts of previous chronicles compiled by the major historical writers of his own century, chief among them being those twin architects of Elizabethan historiography, Edward Hall and Raphael Holinshed. There were several others deserving of attention as contributors to Shakespeare's idea of Henry, but Hall and Holinshed stand out from the herd. What is significant is that no Tudor historian gives anything other than favourable view of Henry's reign and his campaigns in France: even Polydore Vergil, the Italian priest officially commissioned by Henry VII to write a history of his realm, accepts that the French wars were justified, and relays the popular legend that Henry had a vision of a cross shining in the air above his assembled troops after the siege of Caen in 1417, a clear indication of God's favour, and one the historian is inclined to endorse. Edward Hall, whose *Union of the Two Noble and Illustre Famelies of Lancastre and York* appeared at the latter end of the 1540s, drew heavily on Polydore Vergil for his account of Henry's reign, although as a devout Protestant he was more inclined to attribute the king's decision to invade France and claim the crown to the clerical need to divert him from making inroads upon the Church's estates; however, he nowhere suggests that Henry himself had unworthy or unsound motives for asserting his right to govern France.

Hall is able to give a far fuller account of Agincourt than Vergil, by drawing on a number of previous chronicles and traditions to flesh it out. Although, like the Italian, he is somewhat sceptical of his predecessors' estimates of the English casualty figures, he is equally con-

Masterstudies: Henry V

vinced that God was on the side of the English, and that it was to his grace and favour that the victory should be attributed.

Holinshed, whose *Third volume of chronicles* of 1587 appears to have been Shakespeare's chief source in writing his histories, followed Hall closely in describing the events of Henry's reign and in his estimation of the calibre of the king as a national hero. In the earlier version of his work, published in 1577-8, Holinshed adopts a more severe attitude to Henry's youthful wild oats than is taken in the edition produced ten years later, which may reflect the influence of the reviser of the 1587 text, Abraham Fleming. But the fact remains that the portrait of the king is virtually unmodified: Henry's foray into Europe is extolled, as are his piety and gratitude to God for victory; Holinshed does not even voice those suspicions of the Roman Catholic clergy which Hall could not bring himself to suppress. Indeed, Henry on his deathbed is depicted as emphasizing that he only acted on the advice of sage and holy counsellors, who assured him that divine approval of what he thought he ought to do would not be withheld. Whether or not God approved, it is made abundantly clear that Holinshed had few personal doubts as to the excellence of this outstanding monarch:

This Henrie was a king, of life without spot, a prince whome all men loved, and of none disdained, a capteine against whome fortune never frowned, nor mischance once spurned, whose people him so severe a justicer both loved and obeied (and so humane withall) that he left no offense unpunished, nor freendship unrewarded; a terrour to rebels, and suppressour of sedition, his vertues notable, his qualities most praise-worthie.

... of person and forme was this prince rightlie representing his heroicall affects, of stature and proportion tall and manlie, rather leane than grose, somewhat long necked and blacke haired, of countenance amiable, eloquent and grave was his speech, and of great grace and power to persuade: for conclusion, a majestie was he that both lived & died a paterne in princehood, a lode-starre in honour, and mirrour of magnificence: the more highlie exalted in his life, the more deepelie lamented at his death, and famous to the world alwaie.

Such was the paragon of kingly virtues as conceived by the Elizabethans, and such was the image which Shakespeare sought to render dramatically for the entertainment and enlightenment of Elizabethan audiences. However, many of the allusions and much of the imagery Shakespeare deploys in his account appear to derive less from Henry's personal reputation as a monarch than from medieval or contemporary opinion regarding the virtues embodied in the ideal Christian king. When Thomas Hoccleve spoke of Henry as being a 'Mirror to Princes alle' (*Ballad to Henry V*), or Edward Hall referred to him as the 'mirror of Christendom', they were expressing the common belief that Henry's

The Man and the Myth

character and behaviour constituted a pattern of excellence for others to emulate, but Shakespeare seems at pains to bestow on his dramatic hero additional qualities of a personal, moral and spiritual nature, which conform to those possessed by the perfect monarch delineated by the political theorists of antiquity, the Middle Ages and the Renaissance.

Of considerable relevance here is the influential treatise written by the great Dutch humanist and scholar, Desiderius Erasmus, published in 1516 as the *Institutio principis Christiani* (*The Education of a Christian Prince*), with a dedicatory letter addressed to the future Emperor Charles V. The work represents the culmination of a long sequence of similar treatises concerned with the kind of instruction necessary to enable political leaders to discharge their duties responsibly, the tradition being traceable as far back as Isocrates whose advice on the subject was sent to Nicocles, the young king of Cyprus, around 374 BC. The theme may be discovered in the writings of all the major classical thinkers, including Xenophon, Plato, Aristotle, Cicero, Seneca and Plutarch, as well as the Christian philosopher, St Augustine, and a number of his medieval successors. When Thomas Hoccleve came to write his lengthy poem *De regimine principum* in 1411–12 and dedicated it to Henry as Prince of Wales, the ideas it enshrined had been current for something over a thousand years. As Lester K. Born writes in the introduction to his translation of *The Education of a Christian Prince* (1936):

... we may say that the perfect prince of these ten centuries must be wise, self-restrained, just; devoted to the welfare of his people; a pattern in virtues for his subjects; immune from flattery; interested in economic developments, an educational program, and the true religion of God; surrounded by efficient ministers and able advisers; opposed to aggressive warfare; and, in the realization that even he is subject to law and that the need of the prince and his subjects is mutual, zealous for the attainment of peace and unity.

As a result of the undisputed existence of this hallowed ideal, J. H. Walter, editor of the Arden edition of *Henry V*, cites parallels from the *Institutio*, along with passages from a comparable Latin treatise by Chelidonius rendered into English in 1571, to demonstrate his belief that Shakespeare assimilated traditional notions of perfect kingship into his portrait of Henry to such an extent that 'We do less than justice to Henry if we do not realize that in Elizabethan eyes he was just such a leader [of supreme genius] whose exploits were greater than those of other English kings...' Space prevents the citation of every suggestive cross-reference presented for scrutiny by Walter, but a selection will convey in how many particulars Shakespeare's creation appears to conform to the standards of regal excellence approved of by Erasmus and his predecessors.

Masterstudies: Henry V

The cardinal virtue of Erasmus's ideal monarch lies of course in his Christianity, and the Bishop of Ely initially speaks of Henry as 'a true lover of the holy Church'; throughout the *Institutio* it is implicit that the king's responsibility for maintaining the Christian faith must embrace support for those who promulgate its doctrines. Later in the play, Henry is characterized as 'the mirror of all Christian kings' and presents himself to the French ambassadors as 'no tyrant, but a Christian king': the treatise lays great stress on the vital importance of a Christian upbringing for a potential ruler who is adjured in these terms:

Whenever you think of yourself as a prince, remember you are a *Christian* prince! You should be as different from even the noble pagan princes as a Christian is from a pagan.

Do not think that the profession of a Christian is a matter to be lightly passed over, entailing no responsibilities unless, of course, you think the sacrament which you accepted along with everything else at baptism is nothing...

There is no better way to gain the favor of God, than by showing yourself a beneficent prince for your people...

Moreover, a large section of the work is given over to a long comparison between the virtuous Christian king and the pagan tyrant: typical is the advice offered to the monarch who seeks to avoid being labelled as tyrannous by his subjects:

Whoever wants to claim the title 'prince' for himself and to shun the hated name 'tyrant', ought to claim it for himself, not through deeds of horror and threats, but by acts of kindness. For it is of no significance if he is called 'prince' and 'father of his country' by flatterers and the oppressed, when he is a tyrant in fact. And even if his own age fawns upon him, posterity will not...

But it is not enough for a king to be a practising Christian; he should be learned, particularly in theology, and, in this particular, Shakespeare's Henry behaves with exemplary grace, as the Archbishop makes clear in Act I, Scene 1, 38-40:

> Hear him but reason in divinity,
> And all-admiring, with an inward wish,
> You would desire the King were made a prelate.

Nor is it enough for the prince to be concerned to establish the rule of justice within his realm; he must also exercise clemency and be above seeking vengeance for personal motives. Erasmus advises his ruler that 'the affections of the populace are won by those characteristics which, in general, are farthest removed from tyranny. They are clemency, affability, fairness, courtesy and kindliness.' Henry's capacity for clemency is made manifest in the play by his decision in Act II, Scene 2 to pardon the soldier who abused him when drunk, Shakespeare possibly deriving the incident from a similar account in Chelidonius. The king's refusal to take personal revenge on the conspirators in the same episode is again in accordance with approved practice; it is doubtful, however, whether Henry's reference to his control over his passions in the earlier scene with the ambassadors is as directly indebted to Erasmus as Walter implies.

Many of Henry's idealized attributes as Christian monarch appear in Act IV, Scene 1, which takes place on the night before Agincourt; his lengthy soliloquy in lines 23–77 highlights his care for his subjects, the burdensome nature of his responsibilities which lead him to forego the pleasures that his humble subjects take for granted and the sleepless nights passed anxiously contemplating state affairs. Erasmus's perfect prince is similarly described as one 'who is ever on the watch so that everyone else may sleep deeply; who grants no leisure to himself so that he may spend his life in the peace of his country; who worries himself with continual cares so that his subjects may have peace and quiet'. In the same speech, Henry echoes a number of sentiments found in the *Institutio* on the theme of ceremonial, and the flattery which kings have to endure, although Shakespeare's concern is to compare the royal regalia and the attendant pomp with the lifestyle of the meanest subject, whereas Erasmus contrasts the outward trappings of regality with the inner nature of the human being wearing them. In the play, the king's flattering list of titles is dismissed as hollow; in the treatise, the prince is told to beware of all forms of flattery, and to cultivate titles which remind him of his duties rather than those which exalt him in a fulsome manner. Henry's attitude towards his own adulation bears witness to the powerful influence of advice comparable to that proffered in the *Institutio* by Erasmus, and in this supports a view of Shakespeare's hero as the epitome of Christian monarchs.

However, a number of Walter's parallels are less capable of being sustained by a close scrutiny of the texts: whereas it is argued that Henry's willingness to accept counsel from wiser and more experienced men is based on a course of action commended by Erasmus as consistent with ideal practice, the Dutch humanist is in fact seeking to offset the prince's instruction in the theory (rather than in the practice) of monarchy by suggesting that others supply the deficiency. The ideal ruler is not *advised* to seek such assistance. Similarly, the prince of the treatise is not recommended to make himself 'familiar with humble people' as Walter claims, but rather to avoid shutting himself off from the popular gaze, and to appear in public whenever possible to carry out his official duties. The context in which Henry appears as the defender of his realm against the likely incursions of the Scots (Act I, Scene 2, 136–54), and that in which the ideal Christian prince shows himself concerned for the prosperity of his people are very different; nor does there seem to be a very direct correspondence between Erasmus's advice that those who corrupt the mind of 'the best and most precious thing the country has' (i.e., its leader) should be punished, by death if necessary, and the execution of Nym and Bardolph for looting.

But the most telling discrepancy between Erasmus's Christian prince and Shakespeare's dramatic character is found in their contrasting attitudes to war; the humanist takes an uncompromising view of his prince's engagement in military exploits:

When a tyrant sees that affairs of state are flourishing, he trumps up some pretext, or even invites in some enemy, so as to start a war and thereby weaken the powers of his own people. The opposite is true of a king. He does everything and allows everything that will bring everlasting peace to his country, for he realizes that war is the source of all misfortunes to his state ... Let the good prince always lean towards that glory which is not steeped in blood nor linked with the misfortune of another. In war, however fortunately it turns out, the good fortune of one is always the ruin of the other. Many a time, too, the victor weeps over a victory bought too dearly.

Walter is disinclined to cite the passages containing Erasmus's advice to the ruler which say that he should first consider his rights in any dispute and submit them to arbitration: 'bishops, abbots and learned men ... by whose judgment the matter could better be settled than by such slaughter, despoliation and calamity to the world'. He also says that 'wise priests' will deflect the minds of princes from war. When the Arden editor does link Henry's invocation of the evils of war in such passages as Act II, Scene 4, 105–9, or Act III, Scene 3, 10–41, to similar descriptions in the *Institutio*, he ignores the fact that the stage king is utilizing such horrors in pursuit of military conquest whereas the ideal prince is being advised to consider carefully whether he wishes to be the cause of unleashing such terrors upon innocent citizens: 'Must I account for all these things before Christ?'

Such a question in Erasmus brings us to one of Walter's final comparisons, that between the soldier Williams's attempt in Act IV, Scene 1 to pin the responsibility for the human havoc wrought in warfare 'upon the king', and Erasmus's contention that a national leader must weigh up the numerous calamities which will result from his decision to embark on a military campaign:

Shall I alone be charged with such an outpouring of human blood; with causing so many widows; with filling so many homes with lamentation and mourning;

with robbing so many old men of their sons; with impoverishing so many who do not deserve such a fate; and with the utter destruction of morals, laws, and practical religion?

Such are the sentiments of the ideal Christian king; yet, threatening the citizens of Harfleur with the direst of consequences if they fail to yield their town to his soldiery, Henry's sentiments are as far removed from those of the humanist's paragon as it is possible to imagine:

> What is it then to me, if impious war,
> Arrayed in flames, like to the prince of fiends,
> Do, with his smirched complexion, all fell feats
> Enlinked to waste and desolation?

(III. 3. 15–18)

Thus the notion canvassed by Walter and others that Shakespeare's Henry is conceived in the mould of the ideal Christian prince, as set forth in works of political theory culminating in the *Institutio* of Erasmus, needs to be modified to some considerable degree. There can be little doubt that in several important respects, Henry *is* endowed with some of those characteristics deemed to fit the image of kingly perfection. But there seems to be equally little doubt that in certain other significant ways, 'the warlike Harry' is presented as signally deficient in those virtues required of the perfect ruler. If Shakespeare were to draw on the traditional portrait of Henry the warrior-prince, as set forth in the pages of the Tudor chroniclers, he had to relinquish the finest jewel in the crown of Erasmus's peace-loving monarch. Whatever the Christian moralists' opinions, Shakespeare could scarcely disguise the fact that, like Andrew Marvell's Cromwell, Henry V had

> through advent'rous war
> Urged his active star.

Henry in the Playhouse

Given the popularity of English history as a subject for drama in the last quarter of the sixteenth century, it is scarcely surprising that England's most popular monarch should have featured on the Elizabethan stage well before Shakespeare came to make him the hero of his own play in about the spring of 1599. Between about 1587 and 1598 London theatregoers appear to have witnessed several pieces in which Henry appeared as both prince and king. The earliest reference to one of these occurs in a book of comic anecdotes involving the stage comedian and playwright Richard Tarlton, entitled *Tarlton's Jests*, and probably published in the first instance around 1600. The 'jest' in the extant edition of 1638 begins thus:

At the Bull [playhouse] at Bishops-gate, was a play of Henry the fift, wherein the judge was to take a boxe on the eare; & because he was absent that should take the blowe, Tarlton himselfe, ever forward to please, tooke upon him to play the same judge, besides his owne part of the clowne: and [William] Knel then playing Henry the fift, hit Tarlton a sounde boxe indeed, which made the people laugh the more, because it was he.

Since we know that Tarlton was buried on 3 September 1588, evidence for the existence by this date of a play in which the character of Henry appeared seems more or less irrefutable; Tarlton and Knell were actors with the dramatic company known as Queen Elizabeth's Men, formed in 1583 from the best actors from all the other troupes, whose authorized playhouses were the Bull Inn, and the Bell Inn in Gracechurch Street. Whether or not the piece referred to in *Tarlton's Jests* was *The Famous Victories of Henry the fifth* (to be discussed shortly), first registered for publication on 14 May 1594 but probably performed well before that, is uncertain; *The Famous Victories* certainly contains a courtroom scene in which Henry (as Prince Hal) does give the Lord Chief Justice 'a boxe on the eare', but the episode was striking enough to be featured in almost any play in which the 'madcap prince' appeared, where a playwright might seek to capitalize on the legends of Hal's notoriously wild exploits when Prince of Wales.

In about August 1592 in his extraordinary prose *tour de force*, *Pierce Penilesse his Supplication to the Divell*, Thomas Nashe had cause to allude to the still unabated demand for chronicle dramas in the following terms:

Henry in the Playhouse

what if I proove Playes to be no extreame; but a rare exercise of vertue? First for the subject of them (for the most part) it is borrowed out of our English Chronicles, wherein our forefathers' valiant acts (that have line [lain] long buried in rustie brasse and worme-eaten bookes) are revived, and they themselves raised from the Grave of Oblivion, and brought to pleade their aged Honours in open presence: than which, what can be a sharper reproofe to these degenerate effeminate dayes of ours?

How would it have joyed brave *Talbot* (the terror of the French) to thinke that after he had lyne two hundred yeares in his Tombe, hee should triumphe againe on the Stage, and have his bones newe embalmed with the teares of ten thousand spectators at least (at severall times), who, in the Tragedian that represents his person, imagine they behold him fresh bleeding.

I will defend it against any Collian [cullion, rascal], or clubfisted Usurer of them all, there is no immortalitie can be given a man on earth like unto Playes. What talke I to them of immortalitie, that are the onely underminers of Honour... All Artes to them are vanitie: and, if you tell them what a glorious thing it is to have *Henrie* the fifth represented on Stage, leading the French King prisoner, and forcing both him and the Dolphin [Dauphin] to sweare fealty, I [Aye], but (will they say) what do we get by it? Respecting neither the right of Fame that is due to true Nobilitie deceased, nor what hopes of eternitie are to be proposed to adventrous mindes, to encourage them forward...

(*Works*, ed. McKerrow, I, 212–13)

We have already touched on the general significance of a testimony like Nashe's in the first section; in this instance we may glean from *Pierce Penilesse* that the vogue for plays starring Henry had not diminished by 1592, despite the indifference of the moneylending classes. Whether Nashe is referring to a specific play in which Henry captured the French king and his son is not clear, although it could just allude to *The Famous Victories* already mentioned, in which Henry does impose conditions on Charles VI and make the Dauphin kiss the sword, though he does not precisely 'lead the French King prisoner'. If Nashe's reference is taken literally, however, he can scarcely be referring to *The Famous Victories*, but rather to another play with Henry in it.

Evidence for the performance of such a play is found in a work generally known as *Henslowe's Diary*, which is a combined record and account book kept by the most important of Elizabethan theatre-managers and impresarios, Philip Henslowe. In 1587 he built the first playhouse on London's Bankside, the Rose, and here thirteen performances of a play Henslowe calls 'harey the v' were given between November 1595 and July 1596, the company responsible being the Lord Admiral's Men, whose patron, Charles Howard, had commanded the fleet which saw off the Armada in 1588. The Admiral's Men's leading actor was Edward Alleyn, Henslowe's son-in-law. The receipts for 'harey the v' were

Masterstudies: Henry V

dautifying, and when Henslowe drew up an inventory of costumes belonging to the company in 1598 it included 'Harey the v. velvet gowne' and, on another list, 'j [one] payer of hosse [hose] for the Dowlfen', presumably intended for the same play. We have no means of knowing what the play itself consisted of, nor what its relationship was to the Tarlton piece, the play alluded to by Nashe (if a specific text), or *The Famous Victories*.

The Famous Victories of Henry the fifth is the only surviving 'Henry play' other than Shakespeare's, and its earliest performances could predate his piece by as many as a dozen years or more. The unique text which survives was published in 1598 by Thomas Creede, one of the best printers of his day, but, unfortunately, the version which found its way to Creede was not a very reliable one, having been put together from memory by performers who may have been anxious to stage an abridged adaptation of a play they had appeared in earlier. It has even been suggested that *The Famous Victories* is related to the piece in which Tarlton and Knell played prior to 1588, and certainly the title-page of *The Famous Victories* contains the phrase, 'As it was plaide by the Queenes Majesties Players'. However it came into existence, we have to rely on this rather inferior piece to convey the flavour of any original from which it derived, and to tell us something of the treatment of Henry on the Elizabethan stage before his theatrical potential drew the attention of William Shakespeare.

It seems fairly clear that Shakespeare must have known *The Famous Victories* quite well; if it was as successful a piece as seems likely, then he could probably not have avoided knowing it. It belongs to the earliest phase of the development of the English chronicle play, when the playwrights of the late 1580s and early 1590s made capital out of the public demand for patriotic dramas based on the nation's past. There is still some doubt as to whether or not Shakespeare himself pioneered the genre with such plays as the three parts of *Henry VI* and *Richard III*, arguments based on technical matters of dating. What is more important is that at roughly the same time, a number of dramatists began to exploit the theatrical possibilities of English history, usually by focusing on the most celebrated events and characters in the reign of an individual monarch, and blending in some romantic or legendary interest where possible. Earlier in the century John Bale, a vehement supporter of the Protestant cause, had utilized selected highlights from the reign of King John to create a didactic morality-cum-history play, and in Sackville and Norton's *Gorboduc*, staged in the Inner Temple on Twelfth Night, 1561, the outlines of the plot were supplied from Geoffrey of Monmouth's history of the kings of Britain, one of the earliest (and least-reliable) of England's medieval history books. Such pieces did not reckon to provide

Henry in the Playhouse

accurate historical accounts of events and personalities; history was employed to point a moral, religious in the case of Bale's *King Johan*, political in that of *Gorboduc*. But the potential for stage adaptation was clearly recognized.

The Elizabethan chronicle-play in its earliest phase is a hybrid genre about which we generalize at our peril. Certainly in many such dramas the authors were at pains to supply their public with as much variety of incident as might decently be squeezed into one afternoon's entertainment. Of the author of *The Troublesome Raigne of John King of England* (1591), one of the play's modern editors has written: 'He gives us three battles, disputes of monarchs, a coronation, prophecies and marvels, a betrothal, humour in a friary, plots, rebellions, proclamations, the sufferings of innocence, a death-scene, some bombast and satire, and much patriotic feeling.' One suspects that the last element was what really counted. Sometimes it is almost impossible to see any link between the disparate elements that make up the whole of an Elizabethan chronicle-play; the title page of George Peele's *Edward I* (1593) reads thus: *The Famous Chronicle of Edward I, sirnamed Edward Longshanks, with his returne from the holy land; Also the life of Lleuellen rebell in Wales; Lastly the sinking of Queene Elinor, who sunck at Charing-crosse, and rose againe at Potters-hith, now named Queenhith*. And even this hodgepodge of theatrical delights fails to include those incidents which involve the affairs of Scotland, the rebellion there led by John Balliol, the traditional stories of Queen Eleanor's cruel treatment of the wife of the Lord Mayor of London and of her death-bed confession of adultery. Peele may have been groping after some principle of artistic unity – the varied forms of treachery which Edward has to endure as king – but as the most recent editor of the play has admitted, the central feature of *Edward I* is simply 'the jingoistic exaltation of Britain'.

The Famous Victories is typical of the chronicle genre; its attitude towards sombre historical accuracy is fairly cavalier, and in its essential nature it might be compared to the modern strip-cartoon. Its aim is to satisfy popular taste without too much subtlety or sophistication of analysis, to make the figures of history 'come alive' in a racy and colourful manner without too much concern for, not merely the facts of history, but also its basic spirit. Instead we get a lively but vulgar treatment of the period in question, with but one half-penny-worth of erudition to an intolerable deal of entertainment, which has no time for artistic harmony, or human psychology, or historical truth. But before we dismiss it as worthless, we must pay it the compliment of scrutinizing it, for it offered Shakespeare an approach to the figure who became first Prince Hal, and later King Henry V.

Masterstudies: Henry V

Despite its title, *The Famous Victories* deals with more than the Agincourt campaign and Henry as king; it spans the reigns of both Henry and his father, and indeed devotes almost as much space (in its present incomplete form at least) to Henry's exploits before his coronation as to those which followed it. The chief fascination of the historical character for the anonymous author was clearly Hal's legendary conversion from prodigal son to national leader, and so a great deal of space is given over to the sowing of Henry's wild oats, in which he is accompanied by a motley crew of rogues, the chief of whom is Sir John Oldcastle, who derives his name (but not his behaviour) from a historical contemporary of Henry V's who was burnt as a Lollard heretic in 1417. His part in the extant version of *The Famous Victories* is slight, but in this figure Shakespeare perceived the outlines of his immortal comic creation, Falstaff.

The opening of the play is concerned with Hal and his band of ruffians, their highway robberies and their riotous behaviour, which culminates in their committal to prison and their trial, at which Hal boxes the Lord Chief Justice's ears. All this is intermingled with some low-life humour provided by comic watchmen and Dericke the Clown. Henry IV, a somewhat shadowy presence, laments his son's conduct and, confronted by Hal, remonstrates with him to such good effect that the prince is stricken with remorse, undergoes a lightning conversion and confesses his misdeeds. The king soon falls sick, and Hal, finding him asleep in his bedchamber, removes the crown, which causes a further misunderstanding, quickly resolved. At the end of the scene of reconciliation Henry IV dies, and there follows a scene in which the new king repudiates his old cronies, and immediately attempts to establish the legitimacy of his claim to the French throne. He next receives the French ambassador, who bears the traditional insulting gift of tennis balls, to which Henry rejoins, in lines indebted to the chroniclers:

> My lord prince *Dolphin* is very pleasaunt with me:
> But tel him, that in steede of balles of leather,
> We wil tosse him balles of brasse and yron,
> Yea such balles as never were tost in *France*,
> The proudest Tennis Court shall rue it ...

The ambassador dismissed, Henry summons the Lord Chief Justice who committed him to the Fleet prison and, as a reward for his integrity, makes him Lord Protector during the royal absence in France. A comic conscription scene succeeds, in which one of the watch, Dericke the Clown, and a thief are recruited for the war, and the action then shifts to France, where Henry has already landed and besieged Harfleur; the

Henry in the Playhouse

French king organizes his forces and challenges the English king to battle. A further comedy scene shows the French soldiery confidently predicting a famous victory, while Henry is modestly unconcerned, despite the odds and the arrival of the French Herald, suggesting that he make terms. Henry urges his army into the conflict:

> Why then with one voice and like true English hearts,
> With me throw up your caps, and for England,
> Cry S. *George*, and God and S. *George* helpe us.

'The Battell' then is staged, and the Herald returns to crave leave of Henry to gather the corpses and bury them; a comic interlude featuring the Clown and others ensues, followed by a parley between the rival kings, at the end of which Henry confesses his love for the French princess; on her arrival, he woos her as a plain soldier. Dericke is now permitted a scene in which he discusses his battlefield experiences with a fellow-conscript who has been robbing the corpses of the French of their clothing. In a final, formal scene Henry wrings a number of conditions from the French king and the dauphin, including the gift of the princess's hand in marriage. With the announcement of the wedding-day, *The Famous Victories of Henry the fifth* comes to an abrupt halt.

Reading this inept play is a curious experience, particularly if we come to it (as most of us must) after a reading of *Henry V*, rather than before. We have to remember that the garbled version before us is not the original text, but for all that, it is a far cry from Shakespeare's more lucid and streamlined piece, lacking even the remotest traces of imaginative dialogue or emotive poetry. Yet, to do the anonymous playwright justice, his treatment of Henry and others does embody a number of elements and incidents which Shakespeare did not scorn to assimilate into his play, and which indeed he may have been forced to take into account, such were the expectations of his audiences. Moreover, he drew on *The Famous Victories* not merely for *Henry V*, but also, though perhaps less extensively and closely, for many of the good things that are found in the two parts of *Henry IV*.

Whether Shakespeare created the fashion for the English chronicle-play form or merely succumbed to it is not our concern here. It is generally accepted that the three parts of *Henry VI* were among his earliest contributions to the stage; that they inaugurated a new theatrical genre is unlikely but not impossible. Certainly, by the time he came to compose the two parts of *Henry IV* and *Henry V* in the latter part of the 1590s, he had written his own *Richard III*, *Richard II* and *King John*, and seen them joined in the Elizabethan stage repertory by such works as Peele's *Edward I*, Marlowe's *Edward II* and the anonymous *Edward III*,

45

Masterstudies: Henry V

in which, some scholars strongly believe, Shakespeare himself had a hand.

Since another volume in the present series will be given over to *Henry IV*, all that is necessary now is to discuss how far this two-part play is indebted to *The Famous Victories*, and how far *Henry V* should be regarded as dependent on its trio of predecessors. Certainly, several of the characters featured in *Henry IV* owe a debt to their counterparts in *The Famous Victories*, most notably of course Henry himself, Prince Hal – later Henry V – and Sir John Falstaff (*né* Oldcastle). The contrast between court life and affairs of state on one hand, and the urban milieu of tavern and stableyard is effectively conveyed in *The Famous Victories*, and may have supplied Shakespeare with the hint he needed to create, in the two parts of *Henry IV*, 'great public plays in which a whole nation is under scrutiny and on trial' (Kenneth Tynan), although Shakespeare's spectrum is obviously so much more varied and comprehensive, and richer in human observation and linguistic verve. But the conflict between careworn father and carefree son, the latter's association with a 'fat knight' and disreputable companions in roistering and robbing, Hal's miraculous conversion and ruthless repudiation of his erstwhile cronies are palely outlined for Shakespeare's transforming purpose, while in the latter part of the play he found sketched Henry's claim to France, the dauphin's derisory gift, the enlistment of the city riff-raff in the army, contrasts of chivalry and opportunism on the field at Agincourt and the bluff courtship of Kate. Many of these elements were traditional, no doubt, but the inferior play quite clearly left its mark on Shakespeare's trio of dramas encompassing the reigns of Henry IV and Henry V.

It is not always appreciated that when *Henry V* first appeared, many in its first audiences were renewing their acquaintance with figures already familiar to them from other Shakespearean works. In the two parts of *Henry IV* they would have encountered Henry himself, as Prince Hal, enjoying the company of his social inferiors and encouraging their criminal acts, while making it clear that his behaviour was calculated to make his subsequent reformation the more dramatic and noteworthy. Thus Hal's conversion is anticipated by Shakespeare in a way that it is not in what remains to us of *The Famous Victories*. This eases, though many feel it can never entirely justify, the repudiation of Falstaff in Act V, Scene 5 of *2 Henry IV*.

Falstaff, who begins life as Oldcastle in *The Famous Victories* and may well have borne that name in Shakespeare's original version of the *Henry* plays, is still, of course, one of Shakespeare's best-loved creations, and there is no space to discuss all his scandalous yet endearing traits here. Suffice it to say, that Falstaff in *Henry IV* plays an ambivalent role: he

Henry in the Playhouse

considerable, and several recent productions have made great capital from this fact; the hanging of Nym, presumably for a similar offence, is quite casually announced by the Boy at the end of Act IV, Scene 4. Not only does Falstaff receive his dispatch before the expedition sails from Southampton, but even Doll Tearsheet, the vivacious prostitute from *2 Henry IV*, is gratuitously dismissed from the scene: 'dead i'th'spital [hospital] / Of malady of France [the pox]', a remark which several critics have fastened on as evidence that Falstaff, rather than Pistol, once spoke these lines (Act V, Scene 1, 77–8). What is clear is that Shakespeare, in killing off all but one of the 'old favourites' from previous plays, must have had in mind their earlier exploits, and that audiences of his day were no doubt influenced in their judgement of the 'new Henry' not only by the contrast thus offered to his former self, but by the fate of those with whom he once fraternized. The context supplied by the plays discussed in this section may have a central role in establishing our full response to *Henry V*.

Shakespeare and War

'No one bored by war will be interested in *Henry V*.' So begins Gary Taylor's introduction to his edition of the play, and it is certainly true that warfare, its causes, its conduct, its aftermath, stands at the very centre of Shakespeare's drama. There is scarcely a scene or a character in it that war does not touch in some measure, and a substantial number of the characters end by paying war's ultimate price in one way or another. It is of course wrong to dismiss the piece as indifferent to any other concern but this, but in no other Shakespearean play (except perhaps *Troilus and Cressida*) does the business of war play so great a part, or the action depend so signally on the outcome of a single military encounter. It may therefore be vital to an understanding of *Henry V* to look briefly at the notion of war in Shakespeare's time, and at his treatment of this provokingly ambiguous subject.

Of course war for the Elizabethans carried very different connotations from those it bears for most of us today; for us the term probably conjures up visions of muddy mass attrition in the trenches of Flanders, child-victims of napalm bombing in Vietnam, the nuclear holocausts which wiped out Hiroshima and Nagasaki. For the Elizabethans war was not conceived of as something which could involve the entire population overnight, whose images could be brought to one's own fireside, although they did recognize that it might impinge on the lives of those who were caught up in a siege or whose livelihoods might be affected by acts of pillage or requisition. There was also the very real risk of demobilized troops running riot in the city streets, as occurred in 1589, when discharged sailors and soldiers terrorized London for several weeks. But of deeper significance was the fact that although Elizabethan armies included volunteers – professional soldiers, the personal followers of great lords, adventurers and those anxious to make a name,

> Seeking the bubble reputation
> Even in the cannon's mouth,

– the greater part of the Queen's fighting forces was made up of ordinary able-bodied Elizabethans. Such military strength as she possessed derived in large measure from conscripts.

During Shakespeare's lifetime, all males between the ages of sixteen and sixty were liable for military service organized on the basis of county levies. Every summer, annual musters would be held, at which the lord

Shakespeare and War

lieutenant of the county or some other worthy would attempt to assemble the county's soldiery, assess its fighting fitness and provide it with some kind of rudimentary training, probably lasting less than a week. But, as the second part of *Henry IV* reveals only too graphically, bribery and corruption were rife, and often the most unsuitable or unfit recruits were selected for active service. It is clear that at a time of crisis England was ill-equipped to defend herself, at least as far as her infantrymen were concerned. (Horses and armour were levied from the gentry, and in an emergency the nobility were expected to make a substantial contribution to the forces of the Queen.) None the less, it is erroneous to think that the ordinary 'civilian' population of Elizabethan England remained untouched by the wars being waged by the government on their behalf in Ireland, the Low Countries and France, and from time to time on the home front when foreign intrusion threatened. Admittedly, the proportion of the population actually engaged in military combat was probably not more than one in twenty of the adult male community, but on occasion the defence of the realm required many more to muster as required, notably at the time of the threatened invasion from the ships of the Spanish Armada, when well over 20,000 men were deployed along the south coast of England. If one also remembers that the government paid out almost £350,000 a year on its defence budget, and that many traders and contractors, great and small, depended for a living on naval and military activities, it may be seen that warfare and the business associated with it impressed itself on the Elizabethan consciousness in a far from theoretical fashion. Indeed, by the end of the century waging war was straining the country's resources, both financial and human; in July 1601 alone 8,000 men were demanded from the levies to fulfil the military commitments upon which England had embarked. Shakespeare's audiences were thus quite familiar with (perhaps even sated with) war – many of them must have seen active service – and it is far from impossible that he himself served in the army at some point in his career.

Elizabeth's military policy was governed by a number of factors, chief among them England's increasing alienation from Spain, exacerbated by commercial rivalries and religious differences occasioned by Elizabeth's adherence to the principles of the Reformation. This fidelity to the independence of the Anglican Church saw the queen in due course lend armed support (sometimes in token form only) to various Protestant resistance movements, notably to the Huguenot faction in the French Wars of Religion and to the Dutch in their struggle to throw off the yoke of the Austro-Spanish Empire. Her excommunication by the Pope in 1570 gave her enemies at home and abroad the status of crusaders in a

Masterstudies: Henry V

holy war, and as English inroads on Spanish trade routes became more aggressively successful and her support for the insurgents in the Netherlands became more confident, so the dispatch of a Spanish invasion force became inevitable, one of its ostensible objects being to bring England back into the Roman Catholic fold. The story of the collapse of the Armada is well known, but it is not always realized that from 1588 until the death of Elizabeth in 1603 England was still involved in an expensive if spasmodic war on several fronts.

During those years her forces were deployed in various parts of northwest Europe, chiefly in support of the Dutch in the Netherlands, and of Henri of Navarre in parts of France. In 1591 expeditions were sent to Normandy and Brittany, the former under Sir Roger Williams, in whom some have seen the prototype of Shakespeare's Fluellen. Later in the year a larger unit under the Earl of Essex helped Henri to besiege Rouen; in the following year another army under Sir John Norris and Martin Frobisher drove the Spaniards out of Brest. In 1596 a naval taskforce captured, sacked and burned Cadiz and destroyed many Spanish vessels; in reprisal, a second Armada was launched the following year, which led to a partial mobilization of troops in the south to repel an invasion that was only averted by a storm that scattered the fleet when it was two days' sail from Land's End. At the same time, there was a constant need to provide support for the Dutch against the Spanish in the Low Countries, and it was an Englishman, Sir Frances Vere, who in 1601–2 distinguished himself by his gallant defence of Ostend against great odds with a combined garrison of English and Dutch troops.

Moreover, there was always the running sore of Ireland: Elizabeth's reign was punctuated by a sequence of uprisings against English rule, usually headed by one or more of the leading Irish families, often with Spanish backing. Rebellions such as that led by James Fitzmaurice Fitzgerald in 1569 and by the Earl of Desmond ten years later were suppressed with violence and bloodshed. The exploitation of Ireland which followed not unnaturally led to resentment among the native population, and in 1594 Elizabeth had to face the most serious rebellion she had known, under the joint leadership of Hugh O'Donnell and the Earl of Tyrone. It even seemed at one point that the English might be driven out of Ireland altogether, when Tyrone won a crushing victory at Armagh in 1598. It was this mounting crisis which led, on 27 March 1599, to the dispatch to Ireland of the Earl of Essex with a force of 16,000 men, and at the time of the composition of *Henry V* Shakespeare was able to express, in the Chorus's lines which preface Act V, the belief that:

Shakespeare and War

> Were now the General of our gracious Empress –
> As in good time he may – from Ireland coming,
> Bringing rebellion broachèd on his sword,
> How many would the peaceful city quit
> To welcome him!
>
> (lines 30–4)

Unluckily for Essex, he accomplished little in Ireland, and it was left to Charles Blount, Lord Mountjoy, to pacify the country, defeating a combined force of Irish and Spanish troops at Kinsale on Christmas Eve 1601, and then proceeding to lay waste to the recalcitrant colony. The rebellion suppressed, Tyrone surrendered a few days before Christmas 1602.

Ordinary Elizabethan citizens were therefore far from insulated from the nature of war even if it did not directly intrude itself into their daily lives very frequently. But they would have heard of its horrors and heroics from returned relatives and friends, from tavern gossip, from letters, from pamphlets and broadsides, from casualty lists (though common soldiers were unlikely to feature there), from treatises on the art of warfare (if they were literate enough to read them), even from such stage-plays as *The Cobler's Prophesie* (1594) and *A Larum for London* (1607). Thus it is reasonable to assume that among the earliest audiences for *Henry V* were many spectators who knew of warfare at least from second- if not first-hand experience. What would they have gleaned from Shakespeare's treatment of armed combat in this and his other plays?

One of the factors which complicates the search for an answer to this question is that we automatically tend to assume that the attitudes and opinions embodied in Shakespeare's writings will stand out as unrepresentative of his age. Because he is now universally accepted as a dramatic and literary genius, we assume that the views and assumptions he expresses on any topic are bound to be individualistic, unorthodox, eternally valid. Yet as George Bernard Shaw never tired of reminding those who read his theatre reviews, Shakespeare was not an original thinker or a profound philosopher, but rather a wonderful word musician. Even if we dissent from Shaw's tongue-in-cheek diagnosis, it may not do us any harm to accept that Shakespeare's presumed stance on an issue may not always be as markedly unusual compared with that of his contemporaries as we might wish to believe. Moreover, we have to remember that he chose drama as his principal medium, and not autobiography; we should never fall into the trap of assuming that the opinions and attitudes put into the mouths of his characters represent those of their creator. Those who in the past have claimed to catch Shakespeare out in some

Masterstudies: Henry V

inconsistency, say in his attitude to religion in *King Lear*, tend to forget that drama makes most of its capital out of the paradoxes and contradictions which surround the human species.

On the subject of war, the plays appear to contain a number of viewpoints typical of their period and in keeping with the expressed opinions of Shakespeare's contemporaries, to whom military unpreparedness, in the light of England's precarious circumstances in the late sixteenth century, was obviously the height of folly. To many commentators a state of peace was undesirable, leading to slothful degeneracy through a love of pleasure and ease, 'two seducing Syrens in whose beastly servitude too too many are inthralled past recoverie' (Dudley Digges, *Foure Paradoxes, or Politique Discourses* (1604), quoted in Paul A. Jorgensen, *Shakespeare's Military World*, 1956). Geoffrey Gates could write in *The Defence of Militarie Profession* (1579):

When the Lord meaneth to plague a wicked nation for sinne and to translate them to the power and scepter of another nation: then he filleth them with the fatnesse of the earth, and geeveth them peace that they may wax rotten in idleness, and become of dulle wittes, and slowe of courage, weak handed, and feeble kneede.

It is in this spirit that Falstaff in *1 Henry IV* refers to the motley assortment of combatants recruited for the Battle of Shrewsbury as 'the cankers of a calm world and a long peace' (Act IV, Scene 2).

Even the Church inveighed against peace if it meant any relaxation in the constant struggle against the Antichrist, whether identified with the military forces of Spain, the spiritual forces of the Roman Catholic Church or both. Moreover, war was frequently extolled as possessing a necessary therapeutic value for society at large; not infrequently, commanders expressed satisfaction at the size of some bloody slaughter as having rid the commonwealth of 'the very scomme, theeves, and roges of England', so that 'the Realme (being too full of people) is very well ridde of them'. Such an apparently harsh view can be explained, if not excused, by the reflection that gaolbirds must often have made up a substantial portion of Elizabeth's army, and that in 1596 her Privy Council is said to have emptied London's prisons to recruit enough men for Essex's and Lord Charles Howard's punitive expedition to Cadiz. Nor was disposing of the criminal element the only positive function war was felt to exercise: it was often seen as providing an outlet for aggressive tendencies, which might otherwise turn inwards and lead to internecine civil strife. Indeed, in *2 Henry IV* Bolingbroke advises Hal 'to busy giddy minds/With foreign quarrels', thus diverting potential enemies from making trouble at home. Such advice is well in keeping with that offered by serious military theorists, and finds its classic expression in *The Politick and Militarie Discourses* (1597) of François de la Noue where he states:

A great estate replenished with warlike people, ought still to have some foreine warre wherewith to keepe it occupied, least beeing at quiet they convert their weapons each against the other.

Such a view was consistent with those of Machiavelli earlier in the century, and found expression in Sir Walter Raleigh's *A Discourse of War*, where he writes: 'when wars are ended abroad, sedition begins at home, and when men are freed from fighting for necessity, they quarrel through ambition.' Although this particular motive for Henry V's French war is not stressed in the play that bears his name, the presence of Cambridge, Scroop and Grey is there in the earlier part of the action to remind us of the looming threat of sedition; there is little need to emphasize that with their swift dismissal from the scene, the English people are able to unite behind their king. Shakespeare thereby does not necessarily endorse the therapeutic value of armed conflict, but he clearly draws on his audience's awareness of arguments mounted in its favour.

In the same way, he makes dramatic use of the contemporary notion that war had a favourable effect on a nation's morale, stiffening the national sinew, as it were, through military exercise. Shakespeare is at pains to characterize the French as a somewhat decadent and frivolous people, at least in the aristocratic echelons; their talk is of wine, of dances, of fine horses and making love, of the undignified appearance of their foes. Even the Dauphin admits that their womenfolk mock them:

> Our madams mock at us, and plainly say
> Our mettle is bred out, and they will give
> Their bodies to the lust of English youth,
> To new-store France with bastard warriors,
>
> (III. 5. 27–30)

and the Duke of Bretagne agrees that the women see the French as better fitted to act as dancing instructors to the English than to fight with them. By contrast, the English are portrayed as doughty, single-minded warriors who have little time for display or diversions; their unprepossessing appearance, which the French deride, is indicative of their scorn for outward show and their concentration on the only thing that matters: winning a victory against an apparently superior foe. The moral would not have been lost on a country which had defied the might of Spain on several recent occasions, and might have to do so again.

To all this there was of course a religious dimension: there was a belief

Masterstudies: Henry V

that military prowess and success, like so many earthly achievements, could only be assured through divine favour, and that God's arcane purposes might well be served by the gift of victory in battle to those nations selected for special attention. To quote Geoffrey Gates's *Defence of Militarie Profession* once more,

... when the Lord meaneth to advance a nation and to make any people famous and honourable upon earth: he stirreth them up to high courage, and maketh their mindes and bodyes apt to the warre, and in all points sufficient for the pursuite and accomplishment of militarie travaile.

Nor was this all; war might well be regarded as a divinely ordained means of bringing about a political state of affairs acceptable to the Almighty, thus removing any trace of stigma from those human agents who might unwittingly be carrying out God's purposes. Thus it is that Henry can address the citizens of Harfleur almost as if he were an innocent victim of a destructive agent over whom he exercises no personal control; thus it is that Christopher Marlowe's all-conquering Tamburlaine can be regarded as 'the Scourge of God' and the instrument of divine displeasure.

Thus, to the Elizabethan citizen who believed what he was told, war was not seen as an unmitigated disaster for either nations or individuals, and peace was not viewed as the height of human felicity. This does not mean to say that the destructive nature of warfare was not perceived, or that its horrors were passively ignored. The cessation of war (particularly if it were a civil conflict which divided a nation against itself) was doubtless greeted with relief, and the condition of peace welcomed. But the dangers of a permanent peace were also realized; in peace a nation might grow slack and indolent, or it might grow prosperous and so attract the envy of other nations, and this could provoke fresh onslaughts which a people grown too accustomed to peace might not easily be able to resist: 'Neither war nor peace should be expected to exist permanently in a healthy commonweal' (Paul Jorgensen).

It is against this background that we must set Shakespeare's treatment of war in his plays, and in *Henry V* in particular. We may begin by observing that in many pieces warfare is seen as a commonplace, almost a condition of normal life which impinges little on the main action. This is true not only of a history play like *Richard II* but also of a comedy like *Much Ado About Nothing*, where the arrival of Claudio, Pedro and Benedick at Leonato's is prefaced by allusions to their participation in a war afterwards conveniently forgotten, no particular significance being attached to their former occupation.

However, as Jorgensen demonstrates in his chapter on 'The Soldier in

Society', in several plays (*Coriolanus* and *Othello* among them) Shakespeare is sufficiently aware of the contrast between the conditions of war and peace to focus attention on the problems of the soldier returned from the battlefield in adapting himself to the requirements of peacetime existence. Richard III may allude to war as 'grim-visag'd' in his celebrated opening soliloquy, but he also finds peace to be a 'weak piping time,' its 'idle pleasures' irksome, and his point-of-view was echoed by many real-life Elizabethan military men, who discovered to their cost that, in Lord Burghley's colourful phrase, 'soldiers in peace are like chimneys in summer'. Richard III, of course, makes the transition from campaigner to courtier successfully (according to his own standards), but neither Coriolanus nor Othello finds himself as capable of coping with the problems of 'Civvy Street' as he was in leading men to victory in battle; even Henry does not entirely exempt himself from this charge of ineptitude.

It is in Henry's wooing scene with Katharine that Shakespeare exploits the stock situation of the bluff, plain-speaking soldier who claims to lack the finesse which women expect from a gallant lover, and must therefore make love as he makes war, by a frontal assault unadorned by any displays of flowery eloquence:

> Will you vouchsafe to teach a soldier terms
> Such as will enter at a lady's ear
> And plead his love-suit to her gentle heart?
>
> (V. 2. 99–101)

Henry at this point becomes a parody of the uncouth soldier-lover, and his protestations of lacking eloquence ring hollow after his masterly and stirring addresses to his troops earlier in the action. Nor do we believe his self-disparaging remarks concerning the grimness of his own features:

Now beshrew my father's ambition! He was thinking of civil wars when he got me; therefore was I created with a stubborn outside, with an aspect of iron, that when I come to woo ladies I fright them.

(V. 2. 222–6)

It is obvious that Shakespeare here is availing himself of the stock portrait of the military man as wooer, partly under the influence of *The Famous Victories*, and it certainly helps to point up further the central contrast between the pragmatic, no-nonsense English and the more polished but, by implication, more effete and less effective French.

Whatever our doubts as to the sincerity of Henry's performance as a lover, there can be few doubts as to his capabilities as a commander of troops in the field, and it is Paul Jorgensen once again who has most tellingly illustrated from contemporary manuals the perfection of Henry's generalship, according to the ideas of Shakespeare's day. Henry is, in Jorgensen's phrase, 'a handbook perfect officer', whose conduct and speech, where not derived from historical sources, owe a considerable debt to precepts and examples taken from books on military subjects, many of which were in circulation. Indeed, such a model of an Elizabethan major-general does Henry prove to be, that it tends to deprive his portrait of the dramatic light and shade which result from psychological flaws and tensions. Only in the contrast between the cheerful, confident extrovert of the camp and the fearful, nerve-wracked individual who soliloquizes in the night before Agincourt do we sense any gulf between appearance and reality, and the conflict is soon dispelled in the miraculous victory of the following morning; indeed, Henry's anguish serves to make his military qualities all the more laudable. In modern parlance, the king has 'got the lot' as a general : he is merciful to his foes, modest and pious in victory, a strict disciplinarian, never betrayed by overconfidence into rashness, exhorting his men through both the power of oratory and his own example, always concerning himself with the wellbeing of his men and associating himself with them in their peril without compromising his own rank. Henry's copybook-style leadership may be unattractive to those of us who prefer our heroes with a few human failings to offset their virtues and – as we shall see later – strenuous efforts have been made to winkle out Henry's faults and hold them against him, but it is important to grasp that Shakespeare's portrait of Henry as a warrior follows the best authorities of the day in creating an image of soldierly perfection.

Whether Shakespeare intended that image to be viewed uncritically or not is a larger question. It has certainly been argued that in making Henry the ideal warrior-king, Shakespeare denied the character much interest as a human-being, and some have seen this as deliberate policy, a demonstration of the way in which the private individual is swamped by the public icon. This position will have to be explored in its proper place; for the present we may content ourselves with looking at the manner in which Shakespeare treats war from the point of view of those who bear the brunt of the fighting, the common soldiers, the 'base, common and popular' elements in Henry's army. Shakespeare certainly never flatters the rank-and-file , nor, as the Boy's speech in Act III, Scene 2 of *Henry V* makes clear, NCOs like Nym, Bardolph and Pistol, whose main interest is in the spoils of war. Indeed, it must be admitted that Shakespeare's general attitude towards the 'base soldier' is often one of comic contempt for him, yet when one remembers that the majority of

Shakespeare and War

Elizabethan infantrymen were, if not the dregs, then certainly the ragtag and bobtail of the community, his approach becomes at least understandable. One has only to read (or better still, to witness in performance) the recruiting scene in *2 Henry IV* (Act III, Scene 2) to realize the scandalous way in which ordinary citizens were conscripted in Elizabethan England by unscrupulous captains whose concern was simply to fill their muster-rolls, yet one cannot really feel concerned for the fates of Messrs Wart, Shadow and Feeble, who are never presented from any other than a comic standpoint. These are obviously the types of recruit who will make reluctant, incompetent, and insubordinate soldiers, but then Elizabethan choice often lighted on the unfittest.

The same is not true of the men who make up the backbone of Henry V's army: by contrast with most of the rank-and-file in Shakespeare's plays, Bates, Court and Williams are presented soberly, without gratuitous comedy and with some real apprehension of their legitimate fears and scruples. Their encounter with the disguised king provokes a discussion of war from the viewpoint of the average enlisted man who, as Bates and Williams argue, knows nothing of the rights and wrongs of a dispute in which he may be required to sacrifice his life, and moreover to die in a state of mortal sin since 'blood is their argument'. In the speeches of Williams in particular, Shakespeare comes as close as he ever does in his dramas to voicing something of the doubts and fears of the conscripted Elizabethan fighting-man sympathetically: who will take the responsibility, he enquires,

when all those legs, and arms, and heads, chopped off in a battle, shall join together at the latter day, and cry all, 'We died at such a place'; some swearing, some crying for a surgeon, some upon their wives left poor behind them, some upon the debts they owe, some upon their children rawly left.

(IV. 1. 131–6)

Several commentators have pointed out the inadequacy of Henry's reassurances as to the king's responsibility for the souls of wicked men who die in a good cause; Williams is speaking on behalf of those good men who die in an unjust cause over which they have no right to dispute. The fact that Shakespeare here presents a common soldier with a mind of his own, one moreover who is no coward soul (as his quarrel with the disguised king makes clear), is of considerable interest in assessing Shakespeare's presentation of warfare as it affects the common man, but of even more impact in the dramatic world of *Henry V* is the image of that little band of down-to-earth enlisted Englishmen, without illusions, stoically but gloomily confronting the impending battle in the knowledge that they may not survive it. They are perhaps the true heroes of *Henry V*.

Masterstudies: Henry V

It is clearly impossible to explore every aspect of Shakespeare's treatment of warfare, but we have to accept that he was disinclined to take a late twentieth-century view of it as the greatest of all human evils and a phenomenon to be avoided at all costs. This is partly because in Shakespeare's day co-belligerents did not run the risk of annihilating the entire human race if they went to war with each other. Where speeches deploring war are found in Shakespeare's plays, they are often placed in the mouths of characters such as Henry VI, in whom they are dramatically appropriate, but there is not a scrap of evidence that Shakespeare necessarily endorsed them. War was part of the Elizabethan way of life, and perhaps Shakespeare's personal viewpoint would have been that expressed by Brian Gardner in his introduction to an anthology of poems from World War II, *The Terrible Rain*:

War is, without doubt, man's most outrageous activity, and yet it draws from him, too, nobility, valour, and art ...

At all events, it may be worthwhile keeping this statement in mind as we proceed now to examine the play in detail.

Henry V

Text

As general readers, we are not usually concerned with textual matters. It scarcely enters our heads to query which version of a cheap reprint we are being offered by our local bookshop or public library before we purchase or borrow it. It is only when we are confronted with a work of recognized classic stature such as *Hamlet* or Wordsworth's *Prelude* that it may occur to us that there is possibly some significance in the existence of variant versions of the text. Even then, we are unlikely to be unduly concerned unless the specific implications of using one version of a novel or a poem rather than another are pointed out to us. (Or possibly not even then. I once asked a student, 'What *text* are you using?' 'Shakespeare's,' was the disgruntled reply.)

One has to admit that such unhealthy indifference mirrors the apparent indifference of many authors of Shakespeare's period, particularly those writing for the Elizabethan stage in its heyday. Few of them seem to have been concerned about the fate of their draft manuscripts once they had been delivered to the playhouse company who had bought them, and took no pains to see their efforts published in reliable versions that represented their true intentions. Generally, they seem to have been happy to leave it to the players, if they so wished, to sell a copy of the text to a printer for publication in quarto form. Few dramatic writers appear to have thought of doing this for themselves; the printer would normally base his edition on what he received from the playhouse, which might be either the author's original, probably messy, draft (known as his 'foul papers'), or a fair copy of it. (The prompt-book, a copy transcribed from the author's draft by the company's prompter or book-keeper for use in the theatre, would naturally remain in the company's custody.)

Occasionally, however, a printer might be offered the text of a popular piece that did not emanate from a playhouse company at all, but rather from one or more individual actors who had performed in a production of a play and then pieced together a text from memory, obvious imperfections and distortions of the original becoming incorporated on the way. These took the predictable forms of omissions whereby whole scenes could sometimes disappear, insertions of additional matter, paraphrases or garbling of the sense, verse passages appearing as prose

Masterstudies: Henry V

and vice versa, interpolations from other plays, scenes out of sequence and numerous faults of a similar kind. These errors, which can of course only be established by comparison with fuller and more reputable versions of the text, did not all necessarily arise solely from the compilers' defective memories of plays in which they probably played only minor roles: the version they had played in and on which they based their reconstructions might already have been scaled down for performance in the provinces outside London. Alternatively, the players doctoring the original version might have had provincial performance in mind, and so deleted those scenes or passages which would be difficult to present adequately without all the facilities of a London playhouse, or with a severely reduced cast. At all events, it has been usual to refer to texts of Shakespeare produced in this slightly shady way as the 'bad quartos', to distinguish them from those early texts whose publication had been sanctioned by the companies who had the right to dispose of them to a printer.

During Shakespeare's lifetime, therefore, his plays circulated only in quarto form, some of them in quite reputable versions, taken from Shakespeare's 'foul papers' or, better still, a fair copy, others based on the imperfect memories of former actors. Sometimes, as with *Romeo and Juliet* and *Hamlet*, a publisher thought it worthwhile, following the appearance of a 'bad quarto', to issue an improved version, and of course several of the plays, including *Richard II*, *Richard III* and *Pericles*, went through several such quarto editions. By Shakespeare's death in 1616, eighteen of his plays had been published in quarto format; *Othello* joined them in 1622. In the following year, two of Shakespeare's fellow-actors, John Heminge and Henry Condell, gathered together all the plays agreed by them to be his, and so compiled the celebrated 'collected edition' we now know as the First Folio.

Their task was not an easy one. In addition to those plays available in quarto (*Pericles*, though in print, they rejected for reasons it is needless to discuss here), they tracked down copies of a further eighteen pieces, five being in all probability transcribed for them by Ralph Crane (a professional scrivener often employed by the King's Men, Shakespeare's old company), either from 'foul papers' or the theatrical prompt-book. Several texts were taken over direct from the quartos, but many others were created by correcting and expanding the extant quarto editions with reference to 'foul papers' or prompt-books. Some plays (*The Comedy of Errors*, *Antony and Cleopatra* and others) seem to have been drawn from 'foul papers' alone; others (*Macbeth* and *Twelfth Night* among them) from the prompt-book alone.

Heminge and Condell laboured with love to make their edition a worthy tribute to their 'Friend, and Fellow', and the majority of their

Henry V

texts must be assumed to represent the best versions they could lay their hands on or devise from whatever materials were to hand, 'best' being understood to mean those which came closest to what they believed Shakespeare had written some years before. However, time and chance and the needs of theatrical performance had intervened, not to mention the hazards any literary text underwent in the printing processes of the age. Although the First Folio texts are in many cases the most authoritative versions of Shakespeare's plays extant, not only is the edition full of those errors almost inevitable in early seventeenth-century printed books, but not all the versions of the plays created by Heminge and Condell and their assistants are necessarily to be preferred in every respect to those of the quartos, even the 'bad' ones, which often preserve pieces of stage-business left out in the folio text. Moreover, a quarto version can sometimes contain readings of lines and speeches far less suspect in terms of what Shakespeare originally wrote than those which appear in the First Folio. Establishing the precise degree of authority to be attached to the several differing versions of a large number of Shakespeare's plays, which means trying to establish how they came to read as they do, has occupied scholars for several centuries, and seems likely to go on doing so.

Henry V as a text exists in two principal versions, the earlier generally assumed to be a corrupt or 'bad' quarto, first published in 1600 and then reprinted in 1602 and again in 1619. The First Folio text appears far more reliable, based as it is on Shakespeare's manuscript, possibly the one he supplied to the Lord Chamberlain's Men, who first performed it in 1599, although it appears to have been a far more carefully prepared version than many texts deriving from similar sources. The evidence that the folio text stems directly from Shakespeare's manuscript is partly based on the preservation of certain characteristics of his unusual spelling and usual working habits in the printed version. The quarto has never been considered to have anything like the same authority; for one thing, it is much shorter in length, leaving out whole passages, including the vital Choruses between acts as well as the Prologue and Epilogue, and cutting out three scenes in their entirety (Act I, Scene 1, Act III, Scene 1 and Act IV, Scene 2). Some of the more usual types of error are obviously to be laid to the charge of the actor or actors who supplied the quarto printer with the text – it has been conjectured that whoever played Gower and/or Exeter was the player responsible – but it is also clear that the play had been cut to provide a script suitable for provincial performance with a considerably reduced cast list. On occasion, the quarto text can supply a preferable reading to that of the Folio, but there can be little doubt as to which text is the superior one.

Masterstudies: Henry V

However, in recent years interesting new light on the quarto text has been shed by Dr Gary Taylor, first in his *Three Studies in the Text of Henry V* (1979), and then in his edition of the play for the Oxford Shakespeare Series published in 1982. The key to Taylor's argument is that, despite its corrupt nature and its consequent suspect reputation, the quarto version of *Henry V* is in fact derived from a textual source representing a later stage in the play's development than the Folio text does.

Many of Taylor's deductions are too technical to involve us here. But it can be said that in summary form they boil down to this: the original version of Shakespeare's play was probably composed by mid-1599 and presented at roughly the same time – when the 'bad' quarto was published in 1600 it was alleged to have been 'sundry times playd by the Right honorable the Lord Chamberlaine his servants'. The 1600 text, however, was not in Taylor's view simply a garbled version of the original script: the play had, in the meantime, been scaled-down and adapted to be presented outside London by a smaller cast than had originally played it, probably a group of eleven actors, two of whom later 'spilled the beans' to those responsible for the quarto's appearance. The small size of the provincial cast, in Taylor's view, could account for most of the aberrant features of the quarto version: the omission of the Chorus, the loss of some scenes and other changes. But Taylor goes further, suggesting that the abridged text, despite its omissions, still contained some later revisions made by Shakespeare himself, 'either in transcribing the foul papers from which the Folio text was later printed, or as a consequence of suggestions made in rehearsal and production'. Hence Taylor claims that the quarto version has at times an authority which the Folio version lacks, particularly for those portions of the play where the players most likely to have been the originators of the quarto text were present on stage, and even more so where they actually spoke.

In the following, we shall not need to trouble ourselves unduly about the kinds of problems raised by the textual material from which *Henry V* takes its being, but it may help to remind us that in studying works of genius, nothing is as simple as it may at first sight appear.

Structure

In recent years it must have seemed to many who enjoy the status of 'common readers' that the professional literary critics were becoming overly obsessed with concepts of structure and systematization. One result was undoubtedly that some of their number became so dogmatic in reinterpreting literary works that they were forced to distort them

Henry V

before they would conform to some arbitrary pattern of internal relationships or oppositions. Now that the dangers of forcing as vibrant and untidy a commodity as a piece of literary composition into a schematic straitjacket are well recognized, and critics are once more learning to temper dogma with diffidence, the gain in understanding resulting from close perusal of the controlling organization and mechanisms of poems, plays and novels is plain to see. It is all too easy to be seduced by the lively detail in a Shakespeare play into forgetting the existence of the strong framework which usually keeps everything in place.

In the case of *Henry V*, however, doubts have been voiced as to the soundness of the structural foundation on which this particular edifice rests. Dr Johnson in his edition of 1765 was one of the first to complain of what he regarded as 'the emptiness and narrowness of the last act', ascribing what he saw as an inconsistency in Henry's delineation there (former courtier as incompetent wooer) to the fact that 'the poet's matter failed him in the fifth act, and he was glad to fill it up with whatever he could get'. A more general dissatisfaction was expressed by Sir Sidney Lee in his edition of 1908 where he wrote:

> The historical episodes . . . are knit together by no more complex bond than the chronological succession of events, the presence in each of the same character – the English king, in whose mouth the dramatist sets nearly a third of all the lines of the play. A few of the minor personages excite genuine interest, and there are some attractive scenes of comic relief, but these have no organic connection with the central thread of the play.

Peter Alexander in *Shakespeare's Life and Art* (1939) repeats the same accusation, arguing that although

> Shakespeare now shows Henry . . . taking his leave of the public as the victor of Agincourt and heir to all France, the piece itself is a thing of shreds and patches, held together by the Choruses . . . not so much a play as a pageant, with the all-conquering Henry passing from scene to scene . . .

Others too have found this a play 'constructed without intensity', to use E. M. W. Tillyard's phrase.

The question of structure is inextricably bound up with the issue of how well or badly Shakespeare deployed the source materials at his disposal. Johnson clearly believed that he had used up all his data by the end of Act IV (much as William Archer accused Bernard Shaw of using up his plot too quickly in what became *Widowers' Houses*), and consequently had to pad out Act V with inferior dialogue. Lee and Alexander both argue that the chronicle episodes are too diverse and fragmented to provide unity of content, incidents only being interrelated through the

Masterstudies: Henry V

elementary device of a Chorus or a single figure acting as a linking device. To understand the problems Shakespeare faced in choosing his material and then in seeking to weld its disparate elements into a shapely and unified dramatic whole, it may be useful first to consider the sources on which he relied for his story-line.

Geoffrey Bullough sees major debts to Hall's history of the Lancastrian and Yorkist kings (1548), to Holinshed's *Chronicles* in their 1587 version and to *The Famous Victories*, and more minor ones to the chronicles of Hardyng, Fabyan and Stow, as well as interesting parallels with some of the fifteenth-century sources discussed in an earlier section of this book. Whenever he employed the chroniclers' accounts, Shakespeare had to overcome a difficulty experienced by every Elizabethan historical dramatist, of deciding which incidents and figures to include and which to omit from accounts of reigns containing a miscellany of events too various and copious to permit complete coverage. Henry's period of rule was notably brief, but all historians gave space to more than the French campaigns, most significantly to the conspiracy of the heretical Lollards under Sir John Oldcastle (a friend and companion of Prince Henry, but a man as unlike Falstaff as can be imagined). Oldcastle remained an irritant to the king from 1413 until his judicial murder late in 1417, and even led a modest uprising at the time of the Cambridge–Scroop–Grey plot in August 1415, but Shakespeare allows no breath of this to intrude and complicate his narrative of Henry the Conqueror. Nor does he make any direct mention of the new king's zeal in founding religious houses early in his reign, though such acts typified the freshly rooted piety which Canterbury and Ely comment on favourably in Act I, Scene 1. (The two chantries Henry established to pray for the repose of the soul of Richard II [Act IV, Scene 1, 293–5] were distinct from the monasteries.)

Thus, when Shakespeare came to choose 'selected highlights' from Hall and Holinshed for his play, he concentrated on those aspects which had led Hall to entitle his chapter on Henry 'The victorious actes of kyng Henry the V', and left the rest. Having already utilized the colourful legends of Hal's wild youth for *Henry IV*, he was forced to create some kind of dramatic structure out of predominantly eulogistic accounts of Henry's prowess, which offered little by way of light and shade. The danger of finishing up with a monotonous panegyric was acute, and not everyone has felt that Shakespeare succeeded in avoiding one. Not only was he forced to compress 'th'accomplishment of many years/Into an hour-glass' but, more surprisingly, he seems to have chosen to omit many historical facts which might detract from Henry's celebrity. In doing so, he relinquished one way of achieving structural variation.

Henry V

His methods of compression are simple to grasp: Henry reigned from March 1413 till August 1422; Shakespeare's play runs from about April 1414 to May 1420. Though it deals almost exclusively with the war against France, it speeds up matters a good deal, especially the diplomatic preliminaries to Henry's invasion and the steps taken to strengthen the border with Scotland before his embarkation. The campaign details, too, are considerably abridged by comparison with Holinshed's leisurely and more circumstantial renderings, which are expanded by the inclusion of verbatim records of speeches and negotiations, although the dramatist often edited and used the former. Shakespeare's most drastic telescoping of history for theatrical purposes comes after Agincourt so that, with the events of 1415–19 glossed over, the European political context only lightly touched on in the chorus to Act V and Henry's second campaign with the capture of Caen and the siege of Rouen made nothing of, the king's successes can be encapsulated in a single battle and a lone campaign. The exploratory peace talks which preceded the Treaty of Troyes are only alluded to (by Burgundy in Act V, Scene 2, lines 24–8), so that it is the culminating encounter which sets the seal on the action; no reader or spectator will object to that, or indeed to any other device for concentrating the facts to serve artistic ends.

However, what does seem remarkable is the way in which Shakespeare edits his sources in order to iron out any doubts that might linger as to Henry's nobility or good judgement, or detract from the heroic or modest aspects of his personality. Significant, for example, is the author's preference for the lower estimate of twenty-five English casualties at Agincourt, ignoring Holinshed's remark that 'other writers of greater credit affirme, that there were slaine above five or six hundred persons', a figure which would reflect less well on Henry's intrepidity. In a similar manner, Shakespeare's king gives clear instructions after the surrender of Harfleur that mercy is to be shown to the inhabitants, whereas Holinshed and Hall make it clear that not only did the citizens suffer privations before capitulating, but that the city was sacked 'to the great gains of the Englishmen' (a fact later disproved). It is also noticeable that in the play Henry's motives for 'retiring' to Calais after obtaining Harfleur are 'The winter coming on, and sickness growing/Upon our soldiers'; Holinshed attributes the move to Calais to a fear 'least his returne as then homewards should of slanderous toongs be named a running awaie', although the onset of winter and his men's sickness are given as reasons for the return home itself. Henry's piety is stressed by transferring from Hall (according to Gary Taylor) the re-burial rites accorded to the murdered Duke of Burgundy and bestowing them on Richard II, while 'the great modestie of the king' is shown by retaining from Holinshed Henry's

67

Masterstudies: Henry V

order that his dented helmet should not be paraded through the London streets. A further small point of interest is that Holinshed's description of the battle-lines at Agincourt alludes to 'a politike [skilfully prudent] invention' devised by the king:

he caused stakes bound with iron sharpe at both ends, of the length of five or six foot to be pitched before the archers, and of ech side the footmen like an hedge, to the intent that if the barded [armoured] horses ran rashlie upon them, they might shortlie be gored and destroied.

Shakespeare rejects this manifestation of Henry's military forethought, possibly to uphold the portrayal of simple soldiership and reliance on natural superiority, although he does not blench at possibly the most controversial aspect of the king's conduct at Agincourt, namely the slaughter of the French prisoners, which must occupy our attention when we come to consider the play's characterizations a little later on.

Finally, it is worth remarking on the way even Henry's adversaries are given a more favourable aspect than that accorded them by the chroniclers, as if to accentuate the English achievement. Charles VI, although characterized by historians as 'fallen into his old disease of frensie' (and played thus in the theatre, certainly since Harcourt Williams's Old Vic appearance in 1937), is a figure of some power and authority, while his queen has nothing of her historical counterpart's shameless zest for sex and power; the internal divisions between the French nobility which Henry was able to take advantage of are not exploited, though traces remain in the bitchiness among the French High Command on the eve of Agincourt in Act III, Scene 7. The impact of a victory over a divided foe is considerably less than one achieved against a united and worthy adversary.

It would seem that in adapting his material, Shakespeare denied himself a number of opportunities for imposing a dynamic dramatic pattern on it, out of a need to make his hero shine more brightly. He could, for example, have painted a picture of Henry as a paradox – victorious conqueror but cruel foeman, rather as his great contemporary Christopher Marlowe seems to have done with his two-part portrait of Tamburlaine the Great, written around 1587–8. Some critics have favoured such a view, but Shakespeare could hardly escape the pressures, already described, which compelled him to retain the expected image of 'the mirror of all Christian kings'. Those touches of ruthless pragmatism, of humourless self-righteousness which some detect in the dramatic creation as well as its historical original, would scarcely be regarded by many as outweighing the king's virtues, or as constituting more than mere specks on the sun's surface. Nor was Shakespeare interested in setting up a

Henry V

contrast between the youthful King Henry and the youthful Dauphin, as he had done in *1 Henry IV* between Hal and Northumberland's son Hotspur (whose historical age he reduced for just such a purpose). The ingredients for such a clash were certainly there in embryo, from the gift of tennis balls onwards, and Shakespeare (in the Folio text at least) involves the Dauphin himself in the battle, but perhaps he was reluctant to give a Frenchman a leading role in a drama dedicated to the unique qualities of the English national hero. Here then were two possible principles of organization – both involving contrast – which he chose not to pursue.

Not that Shakespeare need necessarily have troubled himself about organizational principles when writing chronicle history. As we noted in an earlier section, plenty of his contemporaries had penned historical dramas without being over-concerned with making what they crammed in fit into an integrated pattern, being content to amass a sequence of striking incidents with nothing to link them, except perhaps the continued presence of the hero, or some vague sense of national identity. Yet we have seen that Shakespeare seems to have been at pains to reject anything extraneous to his main subject that he discovered in his sources, and of course by the time he came to compose *Henry V*, he had relatively unified history plays such as *Richard III*, *Richard II* and the two parts of *Henry IV* to his credit. It seems clear that he was at least prepared to make of his account of Henry V's reign one organic whole. The question was, how was it to be done?

One view that has been strongly canvassed is that in *Henry V* Shakespeare was striving to create a kind of dramatic epic, whose affinities would be closest to the literary 'kind' represented by such works as Homer's *Iliad* and Virgil's *Aeneid*, the great classical epic poems of Greece and Rome. Such an aim was consistent with the Elizabethan obsession with the importance of art in preserving heroic human achievements from the inevitable ravages of time, and Bullough, in printing part of the fourth book of Samuel Daniel's poem generally known as *The Civile Wars* (1595), offers us an account of the ghost of Henry rebuking posterity for failing to do due honour to the great martial attainments of the past. Daniel, whose theme is the strife between York and Lancaster, excuses himself from reporting

> what glorie did attaine
> At th'evermemorable Agincorte ...
> How majestie with terror did advaunce
> Her conquering foote on all subdued *Fraunce*,

but it is quite possible that Shakespeare did set himself this task of

69

Masterstudies: Henry V

commemorating such things in a worthy fashion, and in order to do so, hoped to convert into drama some of the elements of classical epic. For example, Gary Taylor has demonstrated very convincingly that Shakespeare bore aspects of Chapman's *Seven Books of the Iliads of Homer* (1598) – 'Chapman's Homer' – in mind when he composed the famous night scene (Act IV, Scene 1).

The effect that Shakespeare's epic aspirations had on the language of the piece and on its whole orientation will be discussed in their proper places: we are now concerned with epic's possible influence on the play's structure. Certainly the adoption of epic criteria would not preclude discursiveness or an episodic pattern, since these are two of the most characteristic attributes of the form, as even the most cursory inspection of the *Iliad*, the *Odyssey* and the *Aeneid* will reveal, but underlying an apparently fragmentary and digressive surface a basic principle of unification can be found, usually the accomplishment (despite obstacles and setbacks) of some lofty and heroic aspiration, be it a military victory as in the *Iliad* or the *Chanson de Roland*, or the completion of an arduous sea-voyage as in the *Odyssey* or the Portuguese *Lusiads*. Aeneas, called on to fulfil his destiny, undergoes many adventures and distractions, but his ambition remains to establish a home for his people, and in due course he arrives in the kingdom of Latium where he is busy setting up a base for his companions when Virgil's poem breaks off. Shakespeare could hardly reproduce the detail of an epic poem, but the structure of his play may be regarded as following the broad pattern of the genre, with a hero enjoined to fulfil some lofty aim, setting out to accomplish it but being frustrated, daunted, diverted and opposed by turns, but ultimately, through the exercise of sterling qualities, achieving the long-desired goal.

But drama can never attain to the qualities of epic in every respect, and many critics have seen Shakespeare's acknowledgement of that fact by the introduction of the Chorus, a device which Dr Johnson somewhat grumpily regarded as no more needful in *Henry V* than in many other plays where the audience might have been informed of matters they were not to witness for themselves. Yet the difference between these plays and *Henry V* would seem to be that Shakespeare was here attempting something new, a more 'panoramic' presentation of dramatic material than had been essayed on stage up to that point. It is to the Chorus that we owe that curious sense of exhilaration and aspiration which informs the opening of the drama, but he (or she) is also there to emphasize what Homer and Virgil, and Spenser and Milton, were able to devote hundreds of lines of verse to convey, namely a sense of dignity and grandeur, of large-scale effects and wide vistas of time and space, of characters and events conceived on larger-than-life-size principles. The presence of the

Henry V

Chorus reminds us that behind the inevitable 'mockeries' of great events in the nation's heritage – mockeries only because actors are merely human and playhouse resources are finite – there lies the subject matter for 'new immortal *Iliads*', to use Daniel's phrase, and that the pattern of the epic's structure has reference to what the audience is to witness.

But the Chorus can also be used to justify Shakespeare's method of procedure in another respect: the figure can tide us over the pauses in the dramatic narrative, and help to accentuate the structural organization of Henry's progress. As well as being employed as a kind of temporal punctuation mark, the Chorus's appearances coincide with certain phases in the king's slow attainment of his ambition. The Prologue introduces the 'two mighty monarchies' whose rivalries are the principal subject of the first act, at the end of which Henry has made his claim and announced his intention. The Chorus returns to inform us of the conspiracy amid the preparations for war: Henry is to receive his first setback, and Act II shows him coping with it, while the calibre of his troops as represented by Pistol, Nym and Bardolph may also be seen as a cause for alarm. In Act II, Scene 4 we are offered our first sight of the enemy, which is again less than reassuring, so that the act may be said to end in a series of question marks. Are the scrapings of an Eastcheap pothouse, however confidently led, a match for the defiant and resolute French, however arrogant their crown prince?

The Chorus returns to preface Act III with a description of the excitement of seeing an invasion fleet dispatched, and of participating in a siege, but it is clear that Henry now faces his sternest test, of making his martial deeds match his fighting words. If Act II brought threats to his aspirations, Act III brings opposition: Harfleur's walls hear him urging that the breach be filled with English corpses, and the Boy's sardonic assessment of the trio of 'swashers' in Act III, Scene 2 makes it plain that not all Henry's troops wish to die heroes. Similarly unidealized in presentation are the captains: Fluellen, Gower, Macmorris and Jamy, whose principal occupation seems to be disputing on the technicalities of the campaign or squabbling about each other's lack of professionalism. Even Henry himself is tacitly under scrutiny in this scene, and 'the disciplines of the war' are relevant to his performance before the walls of Harfleur. Will Henry have to make his threat good, or is he bluffing? Fortunately, we never learn, as the city yields, but Act III, Scene 5 emphasizes that his situation is still hazardous, and if the French courtiers' gibes do credit to the determination of the English in adverse circumstances, they still tend to suggest a sleek and well-fed cat toying with a plucky but bedraggled mouse.

Masterstudies: Henry V

Scene 6 is hardly more reassuring: Pistol's commendation at the hands of Fluellen suggests a lack of discrimination on the part of at least one officer, and the Folio's stage-direction, 'Enter the King and his poore Soldiers', is a further reminder of the general wretchedness; the king's stern refusal to save Bardolph's life at Fluellen's request is offset by the air of satisfaction at the lack of casualties at the bridge, but Montjoy's suggestion that Henry make terms while he can does not seem misplaced, even if the English leader successfully resists that temptation. Scene 7 with its jocularity and bragging in the French camp does seem deliberately contrived to give the enemy their come-uppance later in the play, but in the immediate dramatic context it seems like another nail in the English coffin.

The Chorus to Act IV is justly celebrated, but its purpose is not simply to paint the scene, but rather to create tension prior to the dawning of the day that is to decide England's fate and justify Henry's expedition. Despite his carefree air and the inspiration provided by that 'little touch of Harry in the night', the king here reaches his own personal Gethsemane, as he agonizes in soliloquy following his encounter with Williams, Court and Bates; the confidence he summons so readily deserts him, and he is revealed briefly as a private individual alone in his suffering. Then he resumes his mask, and goes forward to face the central test of his career. But for several more scenes yet the tension is maintained, until the fortunes of war are determined in Scenes 4 to 7. Then and only then can Henry relax with his comrades, enjoy his joke with Williams and Fluellen, and then switch to consider the lists of the dead. His magnanimity towards the forthright Williams is the gesture of a man who has come through.

Act V is a necessary corollary to what has gone before, although one cannot pretend it has the same dramatic intensity as what preceded it. But one victory, however famous, was not enough to convey to an audience that Henry ultimately accomplished his heart's desire, and was granted the crown of France and the hand of the French princess; these things needed to be shown. The Chorus is thus able to lay stress on Henry's 'mission fulfilled' by describing the joyful reception he received in London, and so prepare spectators for the grand finale, when with Pistol humiliated and dismissed from the scene, the 'new regime' can begin with the hope (ironic as it proved in actuality) that France and England will 'cease their hatred'. The epic progress from the proposition of a heroic aspiration to its ultimate achievement and final resolution has been completed, and each stage in that fluctuating development has been underlined by the use of that unusually employed figure, the Chorus.

Henry V

Such would be one method of identifying the structural form of *Henry V*, but of course it would be unreasonable to suggest that this is the only detectable pattern. For example, Richard Levin, in *The Multiple Plot in English Renaissance Drama* (1971), argues that the piece follows a very familiar principle whereby a comic sub-plot acts as a contrasting counterpoint to the main plot in order to enhance it by comparison or satirize it by parodying it. Levin regards the Pistol–Nym–Bardolph scenes as serving as a foil to the actions of Henry and the English court, so that the episodes in which the trio of pseudo-heroes appear lower the epic temperature briefly as well as offering an ironically unheroic gloss on the mainstream of the dramatic action. The play's structure depends then on a framework of antithetical moods, not rigorously alternated, but depending on meaningful juxtapositions for effective realization. So the mutual animosities of Bardolph, Nym and Pistol preface the uncovering of the Cambridge–Scoop–Grey treacheries; the ardent gallantry of 'Once more unto the breach' is immediately succeeded by the glum reluctance of the comic trio to do anything of the sort until coerced by Fluellen's 'Up to the breach, you dogs! avaunt, you cullions!' (which is perhaps an ironic comment on the success of Henry's rhetoric); the vapid grandiloquence of Pistol is contrasted with the king's genuine oratorical power; and so on. Unity is thus achieved through a sequence of strong contrasts, comic alternation replacing epic attainment as the organizing principle.

Another important set of contrasts exists between the English protagonists and their French counterparts. Here again, scenes set in England and those set in France are not strictly interleaved, but no competent production will fail to take advantage of the hints supplied as to the relative values and attitudes prevailing in the rival courts and camps. Just as Shakespeare contrasts high life and low life among the English or compares the behaviour of the 'top brass' surrounding Henry with the more mundane attitudes of 'old pros' like Gower, Fluellen, Jamy and Macmorris, so the haughty and aristocratic French leadership and the more humane and down-to-earth English command are made for juxtaposition. It is notable that as early as Act II, Scene 4 the French are divided among themselves, king, Dauphin and Constable all at odds, while at the English court Henry holds undisputed sway. The Dauphin is typical in his peevish remarks, and his hurt vanity and waspish tones are inflicted on his fellows in the night scene before Agincourt. The French seem to despise their common soldiery: to them they are 'superfluous lackeys' and peasants, and even in death their limbs must not be permitted to soak up noble blood. The French are all for decorum and show; the English army and its leader pride themselves on their lack of these qualities. As we shall see, this contrast is strongly reinforced by linguistic means.

Another ingenious suggestion as to the principle on which the play achieves homogeneity was advanced by Brownell Salomon in the *Shakespeare Quarterly* for 1980, where he argued that the central polarity in the piece was located in the conflict between the good of the commonwealth and the interests of the private citizen, altruism versus selfishness, the community spirit versus looking after number one and so on. Salomon sees the bishops of Act I, Scene 1 as motivated by private concerns, which are then assimilated into the higher cause of national honour, in which all individual interests will be absorbed. This is in contrast to the 'petty contentiousness' of Nym and Pistol in Act II, Scene 1, a private quarrel taking priority over the greater patriotic one; the same might be said of the conspirators of Act II, Scene 2, while the scene which follows exposes the dishonourable motives of the Eastcheap brigade who enlist for France,

> To suck, to suck, the very blood to suck!

A similar self-centredness is seen as marring the Dauphin's national pride in Scene 4; his quarrel seems to be with Henry alone, whom he despises for his alleged frivolities in youth as much as for his predatory claims.

Salomon sees the Chorus to Act III recalling spectators to the public sphere once more, reinforced by Henry's Harfleur speech, though not by the cowardly display of Nym and company which succeeds it, on which the Boy comments. The group of captains are, however, commended as 'an honourable band' who pool their regional differences for the common good. Henry's achievement of Harfleur is seen as a victory for public values, and Katharine's willingness to learn English is taken as an affirmation of her acknowledgement of the cultural parity between England and France. However, the French aristocracy in Act III, Scene 5 are more concerned for their self-esteem than for their native land, an impression reinforced in Scene 7, so that unity and a sense of purpose in the English camp are offset by jealousies and bragging in the French. Henry shares the afflictions of his men as private soldiers, but in the interests of the public weal; the French fight a personal vendetta and, unlike Henry, show little concern for their troops' welfare. Such an analysis also holds true for the battle scenes, and Salomon is able to defend Act V against Johnson's charge of anticlimax by showing how its two scenes form a diptych in which private selfishness in the person of Pistol is finally humiliated, while the vindicated values of communal harmony are actualized in the signing of the peace and the betrothal of

Henry and Katharine. Even the courtship dialogue, with its sexual badinage, is seen as ultimately contributing to a public communal goal, namely matrimony, the traditional culmination of romantic comedy.

Salomon goes a long way towards creating a unified and coherent structure for *Henry V*, though we are under no obligation to accept his complete interpretation: I have already suggested a different way of looking at the band of contrasting captains. But whichever view of the internal structure of the play we take, there is certainly room for one vital reservation. A great deal of scholarly effort has been expended in recent decades in seeking thematic unity and organic interconnections in many early works of English literature, and very exciting and stimulating many of them have been. But we should never forget that the medieval or the Elizabethan or the Jacobean concept of unity and artistic integrity was not ours, or perhaps we should say they were not those which were sanctioned by classical precepts rediscovered at the Renaissance, but assimilated into English aesthetic theory only by very slow degrees. In the Elizabethan and Jacobean 'stage-play world' a perfectly balanced and symmetrical artefact was often not the goal. The Elizabethans could accept a structure which lacked perfection of shape, where characters appeared only to disappear, where the organization was frankly episodic and unity was only attained by having a single character appear in almost every scene. Unlike Johnson, Alexander and Lee, they did not put too high a value on mere tidiness; nor should we, if we want to appreciate Elizabethan drama in all its aspects.

Language

At the start of Christopher Marlowe's *Tamburlaine the Great*, that other 'mighty conqueror' drama of the Shakespearean era, a Prologue warns us that we are about to

> hear the Scythian Tamburlaine
> Threatening the world with high astounding terms

and the play proper begins with the feeble monarch Mycetes demonstrating his own unfitness for rule through his inability to deliver a 'great and thundering speech'. For the Elizabethans, command of language was a passport to power, and the arts of oratory were assiduously cultivated to just such an end. On the Elizabethan stage skilful speech was not merely a means of description but an invitation to emotional response, and on a colourful but restricted platform lacking sophisticated scenery and lighting, language was the lifeblood of the drama, bearing far more weight than in the modern theatre, where stage-effects are so

Masterstudies: Henry V

much more readily available and speech can normally play a more functional role. But until naturalism set in, if a dramatic character could turn an elegant phrase, build an oration to a rousing climax or move the assembled auditors to tears or applause, this was unlikely to be dismissed as gratuitously flowery or phoney. The Elizabethans valued eloquence in the playhouse as in life, and did not distrust its effects in the way that we might be inclined to do today.

The Chorus's remarks which open *Henry V* make clear the type of dramatic offering that we are about to witness: in the absence of the inspiration of a Muse of fire, an entire realm to play in and royal spectators and performers, Henry's deeds will have to be re-enacted symbolically and inadequately, the actors trusting to the audience's good will and imaginative faculties for any artistic success they may enjoy. Lacking the resources of a twentieth-century director (and it is worth correcting the impression that these are what the Chorus does in fact demand – he does not desire photographic realism, as some argue, but regal facilities), the playwright must perforce fall back on an appeal to the spectators to 'eke out' the performance by supplying what is omitted through such token gestures as 'four or five most vile and ragged foils' attempting to simulate the Battle of Agincourt. Such apologetic remarks not only attest to the lofty reputation of Henry's deeds in Elizabethan eyes – elsewhere stage battles are not so abjectly denigrated – they also alert us to the extremely critical part which language plays in *Henry V*. With access to the components of 'the swelling scene' denied him, the dramatist must perforce proceed to exploit the uses of 'swelling' language to set forth on the 'unworthy scaffold' something of the epic grandeur of this king's personality and his achievements on the field of battle. 'High astounding terms' are as much the order of the day for the Christian warrior as they are for the 'Scourge of God', Marlowe's mighty Tamburlaine.

One of the uses of dramatic language in *Henry V* is therefore to compensate for the discrepancy between the triumphant career of the monarch in actuality (or perhaps more accurately, as it came to be glamorized in historical tradition), and the perversion of it which was all the Elizabethan playwright with his limited facilities felt he could present. This need for 'elevating the tone' of the piece through added stature and dignity may be one of the reasons why Caroline Spurgeon in *Shakespeare's Imagery and What It Tells Us* (1935) saw the keynote of the earlier part of the play in images of swift, soaring movement of which the opening plea for a Muse of fire is typical, fire being the highest, brightest and lightest of the four traditional elements, and thus associated with aspiration and ascent. In the Chorus to Act II, the ambitious youth

Henry V

of England follow Henry 'With wingèd heels, as English Mercuries', an echo perhaps of Henry's own remark a few lines before (Act I, Scene 2, 307–8) that preparations be put in hand together with any other arrangements,

> That may with reasonable swiftness add
> More feathers to our wings...

Indeed, Miss Spurgeon found images of flying birds unusually frequent in the play: for example, the Chorus to Act III begins by observing:

> Thus with imagined wing our swift scene flies
> In motion of no less celerity
> Than that of thought,

and this is complemented prior to Act V when spectators are asked to use their imaginations to envisage Henry's channel crossing from Calais back to England:

> Heave him away upon your wingèd thoughts
> Athwart the sea.

'Fire', although the natural accompaniment of any literary work featuring warfare, is also a prominent image in *Henry V*: its literal uses are obvious, but they are outweighed in interest by at least two metaphorical ones, both associated with soaring ambitions and a desire for success. Canterbury echoes the Chorus's imagery when in Act I, Scene 2 he urges Henry to let his followers' bodies follow their hearts to France, 'With blood and sword and fire', the fire being as much the 'fire in the belly' as literal flames, an inference seemingly justified by the opening line of the next chorus:

> Now all the youth of England are on fire...

Nor is it coincidental that the Chorus before Act V should invoke the 'quick forge' in speaking of the seat of the spectators' imaginations when conjuring up a picture of Henry's reception in London, thus reinforcing the concept of a Muse of fire with which the proceedings began.

But the nature of the language in the play is not to be adequately defined by the presence of a series of images associated with ascent and aspiration. Such images contribute to a much more omnipresent linguistic effect, which has been well analysed by Michael Goldman in *Shakespeare and the Energies of Drama* (1972), where he draws attention to the fact that most of the play's speeches cry out for reading aloud – loudly, if possible.

They are display arias for the commanding actor; they stimulate us to share his

Masterstudies: Henry V

noticeable effort, to be aware of the glory and labor involved in making authoritative sounds. They carry with them, in the most patent and seductive form, the pleasures, the rewarding effort of persuasive, masterful public performance . . .

Many readers of the play will have registered this phenomenon, but what Goldman goes on to observe is less obvious but even more pertinent to this section of the book. Arguing that the physical appeal of the speeches is matched by their content, he remarks:

Significantly, all but one of the half-dozen famous speeches of the play have in common a concern for encouraging their hearers to make some kind of demanding effort, whether of action, feeling, or imagination. These speeches insist on what is strenuous, and *Henry V*'s dominant atmosphere is of strenuous activity. The play communicates a sense not exactly or not primarily of strain, but of straining effort, of life that is arduous, exigent, and sometimes exhausting.

Goldman regards the Chorus, like the king, as a man whose job is to inspire his auditors to unusual achievement, in his case to rouse us to new heights of imagination in order to make up for the so-called inadequacies of staging. Like the Chorus, Henry stirs up the collective imagination of his troops to fresh feats of valour, the Nyms, Bardolphs and Pistols being identified no doubt with those spectators unwilling to succumb to the Chorus's spell. Of the rest, the king demands that they should transform themselves through physical and mental exertion into imitating 'the action of the tiger', and

> Stiffen the sinews, conjure up the blood,
> Disguise fair nature with hard-favoured rage . . .
> Now set the teeth, and stretch the nostril wide,
> Hold hard the breath, and bend up every spirit
> To his full height!
>
> (III. 1. 7–8, 15–17)

Henry's tone is inspirational but the unnatural stress it places others under is well shown throughout the action, not simply through the disorderly trio mentioned above, who make strenuous efforts to appear valiant in order to cover their cowardice, but through Court, Bates and Williams, the typical auditors of Henry's urgent oratory. Goldman shows how even Henry himself is a man under stress: no one can play a heroic part for long without the strain beginning to show, as it does the night before Agincourt. In the morning, Henry is himself again, and reassumes his exhortatory style, but for Goldman the 'famous speeches' reinforce what he believes the play's theme to be, namely 'the demands on the self that being a king involves'.

Goldman's essay is a notable one, but it cannot tell the complete story:

Henry V

the play may abound in images of stress and strain, but our view of Henry is not entirely governed by these. A good deal of the terminology employed to describe him conveys an impression of liberality, cheerfulness and sweetness of temperament: the bishops in Act I, Scene 1 speak of him as 'full of grace and fair regard', and in the following scene as being 'in the very May-morn of his youth', while before Harfleur he speaks of himself as typifying (unless frustrated) 'the cool and temperate wind of grace'. On the night before the battle he looks 'freshly' and conquers his own fatigue 'With cheerful semblance and sweet majesty'. He does seem to possess the capability of making others rejoice in his presence, so that the French king's greeting in Act V, Scene 2 – 'Right joyous are we to behold your face' – and his queen's echo of it do not sound like mere summit-conference platitudes, and make it seem that it is not only the English who pluck comfort from his looks. Sweetness is also one of the qualities associated with the king: Canterbury tells Ely that the royal sentences are 'sweet and honeyed', while Henry's first illustration of the king's mortal nature is to remind Bates and his friends that 'the violet smells to him as it doth to me', an image of fragrance striking in such a context.

Of the natural phenomena with which the figure of Henry is linked, some few are admittedly destructive, as when Exeter attributes to him the authority of some force of nature:

> in fierce tempest is he coming,
> In thunder and in earthquake, like a Jove,
>
> (II. 4. 99–100)

which gives him something of the aura of a Tamburlaine, but Exeter is out to alarm his French hearers, and elsewhere Henry is far more often associated with the sun. This was of course a Renaissance commonplace – Edward III is described in Act II, Scene 4 as 'crowned with the golden sun' – but Shakespeare puts the traditional correspondence to precise use, Henry invoking it in his retort to the ambassadors in Act I, Scene 2:

> I will rise there with so full a glory
> That I will dazzle all the eyes of France,
> Yea, strike the Dauphin blind to look on us.
>
> (lines 279–81)

Here it is the sun's power to harm that is paramount, but elsewhere its effects are more favourably referred to: in courting Kate, Henry likens his 'good heart' to the sun 'for it shines bright and never changes, but keeps his course truly'. This attribution of constancy is matched elsewhere by the quality of universal benison for which the sun was famed being bestowed by the monarch upon his men:

Masterstudies: Henry V

> A largess universal, like the sun,
> His liberal eye doth give to every one,
> Thawing cold fear ...
>
> (Chorus to Act IV, 43-5)

and Williams unconsciously reverses the image in the next scene where he compares a common man's ability to dent a monarch's confidence to attempting to 'turn the sun to ice, with fanning in his face with a peacock's feather'. The linkage between king–sun–fanning is so marked that one is tempted to suggest that in the Chorus to Act III, where we are told of Henry's 'brave fleet',

> With silken streamers the young Phoebus fanning
>
> (line 6)

which most commentators take as a reference to the ship's pennons flapping against the rising sun ('young Phoebus'), the allusion may be to the king himself in the entirely feasible role of the sun god.

The associations of the sun's warmth and beneficence connect with Henry's own reputation for generosity: his eye is 'liberal' in bestowing his favour on all alike – even Pistol can praise his 'heart of gold' (IV. 1.44), and gold is a measure of both the sun's and Henry's largesse, the sun gilding the French armour at the opening of Act IV, Scene 2, presumably as indifferently as it will raise the honours of the English dead 'reeking up to heaven' after battle (Act IV, Scene 3, 101), a further instance of the imagery of aspiration, discussed on an earlier page, honour being considered the product of the fiery element in the human constitution. Henry too is associated with gold as a testimony of his largeness of spirit: he offers those with no stomach for the fighting 'crowns for convoy' and the reward bestowed on Williams for his sturdy integrity is to have the king's glove returned to him filled with crowns. Like the sun, Henry scatters gold generously, and despite Goldman's shrewd analysis, with seeming effortlessness.

But *Henry V* is more than the study of a single character, and the play's language has other functions to fulfil than simply influencing our view of the king. The main subject of the piece is, after all, the confrontation of two 'mighty opposites', and part of the business of the language of the play is to differentiate between them. As we have already seen in discussing the structure of the drama, Shakespeare sketches in the very differing spirits in which the French and the English wage war, to which his choice of diction adds extra point. The language of clothing has a considerable importance here: it is significant that just as Henry has cast off the shallow irresponsible conduct which sullied his reputation as Prince of Wales, so his followers lay aside their 'silken dalliance in the wardrobe' once the French expedition is announced. Throughout the action, the accent is on the English army's lack of ostentation and relative lack of expensive equipment:

> They sell the pasture now to buy the horse,

observes the Chorus before Act II, and we may reflect on this when the Dauphin is extolling the beauty of his thoroughbred steed in Act III, Scene 7. In the same manner, the Constable's observation which launches that scene, that he has 'the best armour in the world', contrasts with the 'war-worn coats' in which the English sit by their watchfires like 'So many horrid ghosts' (Chorus to Act IV). Henry himself admits to Montjoy that his troops do not make a very pleasing aesthetic picture:

> Our gayness and our gilt are all besmirched
> With rainy marching in the painful field.
> There's not a piece of feather in our host –
>
> (IV. 3. 110–12)

so that it seems to the French a further insult for such an 'ill-favoured' army to be taking the field against them. 'Can't they spruce themselves up a bit before we annihilate them?' is the tenor of the Dauphin's scornful suggestion:

> Shall we go send them dinners, and fresh suits,
> And give their fasting horses provender,
> And after fight with them?
>
> (IV. 2. 55–7)

One can hear the social superiority in his voice: 'You'd have thought they'd have made a bit of an *effort*,' would be its present-day counterpart. It goes with Montjoy's horrified qualm after the battle that many of the French princes

> Lie drowned and soaked in mercenary blood;
> So do our vulgar drench their peasant limbs
> In blood of princes...
>
> (IV. 7. 74–6)

to which Henry's professedly democratic sentiment in Act IV, Scene 3 is in marked contrast:

> For he today that sheds his blood with me
> Shall be my brother; be he ne'er so vile,
> This day shall gentle his condition...
>
> (lines 61–3)

Other speeches highlight the contrast between the outward appearances

Masterstudies: Henry V

of the rival armies, employing the imagery of dress once more to register the point:

> ... my poor soldiers tell me, yet ere night
> They'll be in fresher robes, or they will pluck
> The gay new coats o'er the French soldiers' heads,
> And turn them out of service ...
>
> (IV. 3. 116–19)

The Constable having commended the French knights for their 'fair show' in the previous scene, the inference is that the French should have paid less attention to externals, 'gay new coats' and so on, and more to the actual calibre of their fighting men; the Dauphin's final reference to feathered finery in Act IV, Scene 5 is very apt:

> Reproach and everlasting shame
> Sits mocking in our plumes.
>
> (lines 4–5)

It is a well-tried formula in entertainment and popular literature to bring the unfancied team off the field as the victors; here the battle goes to the scruffy unit with the rusty helmets and the rough tongues, not the brigade with the nattiest gear and the smooth line in talk.

Much of the language of *Henry V* must inevitably be that of battle and warfare, and Paul Jorgensen in the first chapters of *Shakespeare's Military World* demonstrates how Shakespeare's descriptions usually follow the approved Renaissance precepts for presenting (in Canterbury's words),

> A fearful battle rendered you in music.
>
> (I. 1. 44)

Through sound imagery the dramatist builds up on hallowed principles a vivid portrait of the ancient war-machine in action in several of his plays. However, it is notable that warfare and battle are more talked about than actually presented, partly no doubt the result of the limited means at the playwright's disposal for actually enacting a famous clash of arms on stage, although action with no accompanying dialogue must also have played a part. Through the use of military instruments – trumpets, fifes and drums – whose professional usage Shakespeare seems to comprehend, and by employing the musical affiliations of warfare, his dramas present armed combat with all the requisite atmosphere and grandeur expected by Renaissance spectators, without always resorting to abortive attempts at realistically convincing representation.

It therefore comes as something of a shock to realize that *Henry V* contains very few direct descriptions of actual fighting; there are no grand, set-piece delineations of battles, no poetic narratives of attacks and skirmishes; indeed, for Agincourt itself, Shakespeare appears to have relied on the ragged foils 'in brawl ridiculous' to do service for one of the most celebrated feats of arms in English history. The most memorable single descriptive passage involves, not armies in conflict, but armies at rest in camp at night, the implication behind the Chorus to Act IV being that there is a kind of communal experience in war which unites friend and foe.

Elsewhere, it is interesting to note Shakespeare's technique for infusing his play with a warlike dimension without recourse to battle descriptions. Recollections of Edward III's victory at Crécy are invoked by both English and French courts, thereby associating Henry's campaign with former successes in arms, to which he himself appeals before Harfleur, when he reminds his troops that their

> blood is fet [derived] from fathers of war-proof! –
> Fathers that, like so many Alexanders,
> Have in these parts from morn till even fought.
>
> (III. 1. 18–20)

War in such contexts is idealized, and it is significant that the only detailed descriptions of individual deaths, those of Suffolk and York in IV.6, are similarly romanticized, which renders them less harrowing. By contrast, Williams's more realistic picture in Act IV, Scene 1 does not minimize the nightmarish horror of 'all those legs, and arms, and heads, chopped off in a battle'.

Shakespeare in Henry's speeches tends to lay more emphasis on the sufferings of the non-combatants than he does on those of the soldiery: in challenging the Dauphin in Act I, Scene 2, Henry paints for the ambassadors a graphic vision of the woes of widows and mothers, a line he is not slow to exploit before Harfleur, where his target is the civilian population of the town. He conjures up a vista of military anarchy where virgins, infants and senior citizens are most at risk, and this emphasis on the innocent victims of combat is made the corollary of Henry's urgings on the town walls that his troops should not dishonour their parents. The image of a brutal and licentious soldiery barely held in check is horrifying, and even if contradicted both by what we see of the troops themselves and by Henry's reputation as a disciplinarian, its gruesome details have the desired effect.

Whether or not we are to see Henry's threats as idle or not, their keynote accords well with the concept of war as some kind of natural phenomenon, which is found throughout the play. An attack across the

Masterstudies: Henry V

border by the Scots is likened in Act I, Scene 2 to the tide pouring in to a breach in a dyke, the French king compares the English approach to waters swirling into a whirlpool (II. 4. 9–10), while some lines later, Exeter invokes tempest, thunder and earthquake to terrorize the court. Later the King of France compares his defending army to melted snow rushing down the alpine valleys, while Henry's images are often of war as some kind of monster, personifying it at one point as a fiend 'Array'd in flames' with a 'smirched complexion'. Earlier on, Exeter also visualizes war as a monster with 'vasty jaws', hungry for prey, a concept paralleled in the Chorus to Act III by the 'fatal mouths' of the cannons 'gaping on girded Harfleur'. Even the very troops are urged to transform themselves into ugly monsters, their eyes protruding from their heads in imitation of 'the brass cannon', an image in which some critics find an element of grotesque humour.

As the action advances, so a less dramatic and heroic vision of warfare emerges; initially war may thrill and excite, but for Henry's rain-sodden and disheartened forces, to whom the epithet 'poor' is frequently applied in Act IV, it is a wretched and unglamorous business, which even Henry's cheerfulness and personal resilience cannot totally transform. 'The royal Captain of this ruined band' is now given lines which suggest almost a kind of desperation, as when he assures Montjoy that even if the English die in France and are buried there, the sun will draw the stench out and so poison the French climate that slaughter will still result. The forlorn army, skeletal and shivering, typifies all those ravages of war that do not result from the business of fighting; their plight is even extended to their horses:

> their poor jades
> Lob down their heads, dropping the hides and hips,
> The gum down-roping from their pale-dead eyes,
> And in their pale dull mouths the gimmaled [hinged] bit
> Lies foul with chawed grass, still and motionless...
>
> (IV. 2. 44–8)

This remarkable passage offers a realistic gloss on the confident tone of the initial Chorus, where spectators were urged to think of horses,

> Printing their proud hoofs i'th'receiving earth.

The slaughter of the French prisoners, Montjoy's poignant description of the mangled French dead, contribute to the accumulation of detail which renders a lengthy descriptive rendition of Agincourt unnecessary, but leads by a natural progression to Burgundy's account of the disruption war has wrought to normal life, and from the arts of peace have

Henry V

been brought to a standstill. Conflict has invaded the world of nature, and we are parties to the survival of the roughest and rudest since

> nothing teems
> But hateful docks, rough thistles, kecksies, burs...
>
> (V. 2. 51–2)

The picture of perverted nature is a frequent one in Shakespeare, and the intensely charged diction employed here is the counterpart to the language of warfare which has dominated so much of the action.

Shakespeare's reluctance to provide his play with a series of set-piece depictions of battle is not echoed elsewhere. Indeed, *Henry V* contains an unusually high proportion of such oratorical arias for a play written at this period in its author's career. Such speeches do not always grow completely naturally out of the context, or else seem to be built on rather more ample lines than the situation warrants. Modern taste in such matters notwithstanding, and leaving out of account the Choruses, which have a special function, there are four speeches which might be regarded as too easily separable from the texture of the play to be left undiscussed. The easiest to justify from a dramatic standpoint is Henry's soliloquy on ceremony, which occupies the central position in Act IV, Scene 1: it does not follow logically from what has gone before, in the sense that the king has not so far been seen as the victim of adulation or flattery, or likely to be corrupted by them. It is a speech which could be legitimately placed in the mouth of any of Shakespeare's kings with equal effectiveness, but because it is skilfully connected to Henry's overburdening sense of responsibility and his wakefulness while his subjects sleep, its somewhat formal, detached quality is overlooked. More incongruous and prolix would seem to be Henry's lengthy discourse on treason with which he torments Cambridge, Scroop and Grey before dismissing them to their deaths. Its frequent recourse to stock imagery, particularly that of demonic lore, and rhetorical tropes of the type Shakespeare loved to employ in earlier works such as *Henry VI* and *Richard III*, suggests a lowering of imaginative pressure here; though the Elizabethan abhorrence of treachery perhaps lies behind the lines, for many readers they labour the points in a tedious and inartistic fashion.

The other speeches which create problems of reception today are both given to the Archbishop in Act I, Scene 1; one is the celebrated (if inaccurate) analogy between the conduct of a beehive and the smooth running of a kingdom, which has often been seized on as Shakespeare's endorsement of Tudor governmental theory, and which, like the epic similes of Homer, Virgil and Milton, is doubtless introduced to supply a little respite and relief in a scene with a predominantly political flavour. Less easy to interpret are the sixty-odd lines in which Canterbury takes it

Masterstudies: Henry V

upon him to explain Salic law and its dubious application to his sovereign and the assembled peers (I. 2. 33–95). Some of the varying interpretations of the *dramatic* significance of the speech will be aired shortly, but for the present it is the *language* of the lines which must occupy us. Like a number of the more factual passages in the play, the Archbishop's arguments are modelled very closely on the treatment of the same information in the pages of Holinshed. The register employed is deliberately dry and legalistic, as befits the nature of the situation: Henry's right to claim the throne of France through descent from the female line is in question, and the lawyer's language in which the speech is couched is of paramount importance to emphasize that legality. The roll-call of names and dates may seem needlessly detailed, but the manner is almost inevitable in the circumstances. The inordinate length is another matter.

However, these speeches are not the only passages in the play which contain clearly visible (or audible) rhetorical devices: some of the most noticeable do have the effect of making parts of the piece seem rather old-fashioned, reminders of earlier works such as *Romeo and Juliet* or *Love's Labour's Lost*, where Shakespeare seems to revel in the self-conscious artistry of such formal techniques. As he developed he 'loosened the structures' as S. S. Hussey puts it in *The Literary Language of Shakespeare* (1982); in *Henry V*, some of the structures would appear to have tightened up again. A notable instance occurs in the speech on treason just alluded to; Scroop's treachery is highlighted in a series of rhetorical queries, answered in identical phrases:

> Show men dutiful?
> Why, so didst thou. Seem they grave and learnèd?
> Why, so didst thou. Come they of noble family?
> Why, so didst thou. Seem they religious?
> Why, so didst thou ...

(II. 2. 127–31)

The effect is slightly incantatory, like an inquisition or a religious ritual, but within the context of a more naturalistic style, such devices seem incongruous. But then the whole sequence is marked by a greater degree of formalism than elsewhere, as the orchestrated confessions of the three traitors in succession confirm. The king's pronouncement of sentence also follows an ascending path, not unlike some of Thomas Kyd's carefully designed cadences in one of the earliest Elizabethan stage successes, *The Spanish Tragedy*:

> ... you would have sold your king to slaughter,
> His princes and his peers to servitude,

Henry V

> His subjects to oppression and contempt,
> And his whole kingdom into desolation.
>
> (II. 2. 170–3)

Similar devices can be detected in Montjoy's frigidly structured announcement in Act III, Scene 6; whether their purpose is to raise a smile is unclear, but the carefully outraged phrases in triplicate might suggest as much:

> England shall repent his folly, see his weakness, and admire our sufferance ... the losses we have borne, the subjects we have lost, the disgrace we have digested ...
>
> (lines 122–3, 124–6)

smacks more of Sir Andrew Aguecheek's challenge in *Twelfth Night* than that of a serious foeman. It certainly helps to underline the impression of affectation already noted in the French.

Prose does not play a central part in *Henry V*, but its usage is of great interest in assessing the play's diction; it is, for example, the medium in which most of the non-aristocratic characters express themselves, Pistol excluded. (He speaks a brand of antiquated fustian derived from Elizabethan popular drama.) The use of prose permits a more informal tone to pervade certain scenes where it is necessary to moderate the play's usually elevated manner in favour of the colloquial language of common life, and to displace the heroic note by one of comedy. For one thing, Shakespeare's prose idiom allows him to mimic more directly than in verse the cadence of ordinary conversation, with all its clichés, repetitions, *non sequiturs* and homely images, its anecdotal and proverbial touches. Nym's speeches in Act II, Scene 1 are the first to undercut the prevailing mood of epic endeavour and introduce a sense of human scale after the glaring confrontation of 'two mighty monarchies'. His quarrel with Pistol not only offers a small-scale conflict which is personal enough to comprehend, but Nym's replies to Bardolph's anxious queries are full of the linguistic detritus that clogs up the everyday remarks most of us perpetuate:

> I cannot tell; things must be as they may. Men may sleep, and they may have their throats about them at that time, and some say knives have edges: it must be as it may – though patience be a tired mare, yet she will plod – there must be conclusions – well, I cannot tell.
>
> (lines 19–23)

One would need to turn to Harold Pinter for as good an example of the humour that can arise from English as She is Spoke.

This more unbuttoned manner works well too in differentiating one

Masterstudies: Henry V

character from another: Brian Vickers in *The Artistry of Shakespeare's Prose* (1968) observes that *Henry V* is the last play in which the playwright relies on stock regional dialects and the use of catch-phrases to identify his creations before moving on to coin more individualized styles, but none the less his use of these Dickensian devices is masterly, from the confident malapropisms of Mistress Quickly to the Irishisms of Macmorris, the Scots of Jamy and, most delightful of all, the Welsh–English of Fluellen. Linguistically, Fluellen is not only memorable for his faulty command of the language – stage Welshmen were not uncommon at this period – but for his pedantry and love of proliferating categories, as befits an ardent student of 'the disciplines of the war', to which his rebuke to Gower witnesses:

... you shall find, I warrant you, that there is no tiddle-taddle nor pibble-babble in Pompey's camp. I warrant you, you shall find the ceremonies of the wars, and the cares of it, and the forms of it, and the sobriety of it, and the modesty of it, to be otherwise.

(IV. 1. 69–74)

It is noteworthy that Shakespeare does not bestow regional idiosyncrasies on the trio of soldiers who accost the king on the eve of Agincourt: their purpose is not to provide comic relief, but to bring another facet of the war to our (and Henry's?) notice.

If prose is the medium generally reserved for the plebeian characters, it is also the medium which the more patrician figures adopt at certain points in the action. Occasionally it is used to sustain a more relaxed atmosphere, as in Act III, Scene 4, where it would be almost impossible to mount the English lesson which Alice gives Katharine if it were couched in verse. Similarly, the pre-battle girding and sexual jesting between the French nobles would not lend itself naturally to poetic treatment; as Vickers remarks, their 'petty quibbling prose' is precisely what the scene requires if it is to expose the dissension among the French leadership.

But of course the chief aristocrat to put verse aside and use plain prose is the king himself, who adopts it when talking incognito with his soldiers, in conversing with Fluellen in Act III, Scene 6 and with Williams and Fluellen in Act IV, Scene 7. Prose here helps to characterize Henry the good mixer, Henry the soldier's friend, although his speeches in defence of 'the king' to Williams, Bates and Court are carefully structured and worded to maintain regal authority, even when shrouded in disguise. The king's speeches may adopt a more naturalistic style along with Sir Thomas Erpingham's cloak, but he remains a dominant figure even divested of the 'ceremonies' of his poetic idiom.

Henry V

Most interesting of all, Henry's assumptions of the common man's garb of prose is found in his courtship of Kate in the final scene; as one speaker of royal blood addressing another, Henry might be expected to use poetry for his amorous diplomacy, but the choice of prose was wise for several reasons. For one thing, as we have seen, the comedy of the encounter is more easily sustained in the less intensive idiom, while prose still permits Shakespeare to create an elegant and witty style consistent with Henry's bantering, self-denigrating approach to his future bride. Moreover, the use of prose is consistent with Henry's presentation of himself as a bluff, uncultured, plain-speaking soldier (however spurious the self-portrait he paints). To woo Kate in poetry would doubtless seem to Henry in this role as an act of self-betrayal; his adopted mood at this juncture is not unlike that of John Donne when he wrote:

> I am two fools, I know,
> For loving, and for saying so
> In whining poetry ...
>
> 'The Triple Fool'

But being Henry, Shakespeare cannot prevent his prose from being more accomplished and effective in its persuasive capacity than any other character's in the drama. Henry may set aside his use of verse in his informal, off-duty moments, but Canterbury's commendation of his 'sweet and honeyed sentences' applies no less to the king's command of the 'everyday' medium of prose than to his loftiest flights of inspirational poetic oratory.

Characterization

In academic circles, it is all too common nowadays to scoff at essay questions of the 'Write a character study of Falstaff/Hamlet/Caliban' type, which tend to suggest we can discuss dramatic figures as if they always behave like real people. Such an approach is associated with a literary period when the kind of naturalistic psychology found in the late nineteenth-century novel held sway, and A. C. Bradley's *Shakespearean Tragedy* provided the tragic heroes and villains with convincingly coherent case-histories. Yet although the figures of Elizabethan drama cannot be analysed in this way: not every speech or action can be taken as revelatory of character, as Malcolm Kelsall reminds us in his excellent brief introduction, *Studying Drama* (1985), performers in drama need *something* to impersonate, or they cannot create a role:

The actor has got to move, to speak, even to give an impression of thought (the sub-text). Unless there is somebody there to impersonate, nothing is going to

Masterstudies: **Henry V**

happen. Plays are not oratorios in which the singers stand still. They are not like announcements of plane departures in which tone of voice, emotion, personal motivation are irrelevant.

But as Kelsall goes on to demonstrate, in Shakespeare and other playwrights, dramatic speech must frequently combine characterization with other functions: it may bring out the thematic concerns of the play; it may supply the audience with vital information; it may establish a play's predominant genre (comedy or tragedy, say); it may help to create the piece's stylistic register. Let us take, for instance, Exeter's threatening words at the French court when he arrives there as Henry's ambassador in Act II, Scene 4. The king's uncle has to adopt the mode of his nephew in addressing the French king and his nobles, speaking not as a character in his own right, but rather as Henry's mouthpiece: 'This is what the King of England would say if he were here,' seems to be his attitude. He also echoes the tenor of the Archbishop's defence of the English right to the throne of France:

> 'Tis no sinister nor no awkward claim
> Picked from the worm-holes of long-vanished days,
> Nor from the dust of old oblivion raked...
>
> (lines 85–7)

and the fact that he is a kind of 'elder statesman', of a generation prior to Henry's own, gives extra weight to the invocation of Edward III and the impeccable pedigree through which the throne of France is declared to be forfeit. Having formally announced the grounds of his argument, Exeter is then free to conjure up a picture of the projected assault on Charles VI's kingdom, and to convey his personal reaction to the Dauphin's mocking present: even then, in doing so he employs the tone of Henry's speeches in Act I, Scene 2.

How much of the 'character' of Exeter emerges from all this? On the printed page, perhaps not so very much; the impression is ostensibly that what Exeter says could be communicated over the theatre's public address system without much loss. But it is not difficult to imagine how an actor playing Exeter could 'personalize' the English peer, and indeed how he must do so if he is going to extract a playable stage part from the lines. A trained actor will be scanning his words (and those of others) for opportunities for emphasis, reaction, movement, facial and bodily gesture, to coordinate them into a convincing portrayal of a human being rather than a mere robot equipped with a speaking device. Then there will be the matter of how Exeter should conduct himself at a foreign court. Perhaps with deference at first, then with increasing scorn for those who will not accept the inevitable. Should he stress such phrases as

Henry V

'the borrowed glories' (line 79)? How should he handle his later admission that Henry is a changed man – proudly, contemptuously or with a touch of humour? Should he adopt a different tone in addressing the Dauphin – bluff, grizzled warrior confronting dandified stripling? Is he angry or amused? Of course, in performing this scene the player will take into account the other episodes in which Exeter appears, but he will expect the script to help him create a 'character'.

The moral is surely that we cannot afford to leave characterization out of account in assessing any drama: what we must always do, however, is remember that playwrights do not write plays simply or exclusively to reveal human personality, and that dramatic dialogue has many other demands made on it in the course of a dramatic action. But it would be foolish to forget that one of the pleasures we take in theatrical representations is that of seeing patterns of human behaviour work themselves out before us, or of enjoying the spectacle of figures whom we recognize as resembling ourselves in sufficient measure to arouse our interest, sympathy, or antipathy.

To say that *Henry V* is not particularly rich in characterizations of a vivid kind may seem uncharitable to a work which includes the lively vignettes of Pistol, Nym, and Fluellen, yet by comparison with the two parts of *Henry IV* (even if we discount the unrepeatable role of Falstaff), *Henry V* appears deficient in this area. The cast list seems dominated by long lines of peers both French and English –

> Bedford and Exeter,
> Warwick and Talbot, Salisbury and Gloucester

– and although a few of these can be made to stand out from the crowd (the English Exeter and the French Constable must be considered the meatier roles among the courtiers), most of them make no real claims to be considered as 'characters' in the novelistic sense of the term. Moreover, this is a play in which figures appear only to disappear, and it is typical that the only member of the 'Eastcheap five' to make any kind of an exit is Pistol: the untimely ends of Nym and Bardolph are only reported (in the text at any rate – some recent productions have shown the execution of Bardolph); the Boy is slaughtered along with the other baggage guards; Mistress Quickly is not referred to after Act II, Scene 3, unless Pistol's reference in Act V, Scene 1 to 'my Doll is dead i' th' spital [hospital] / Of malady of France [pox]' should be amended as Johnson maintained to 'Nell' (even if the method of departure seems more appropriate to Doll Tearsheet, the generous whore of *2 Henry IV*). But the same cavalier authorial attitude prevails with many other characters: Canterbury and Ely might reasonably have reappeared in Act V, Scene 2;

91

Masterstudies: Henry V

the Dauphin plays no further part after the humiliation of Agincourt; a last glimpse of Macmorris and Jamy when Fluellen avenges himself on Pistol could have brought the discourse 'concerning the disciplines of the war' to some kind of comic conclusion. This is not to argue that many of these parts cannot be made pleasing in performance, merely that they are in many cases unfinished and offer a performer few chances for rounding them off satisfactorily.

So much critical attention having been given to the personality with which the dramatist endowed Henry, it may be refreshing to begin a discussion of the character-drawing by setting the leading figure aside and looking at his satellites, for there can be little doubt that the subsidiary roles have been far less subject to controversy than that of the king. The only possible competitor in terms of theatrical centrality is the apparent non-character of the Chorus, but even he in performance proves to be a distinct personality, despite his ostensibly impersonal position, and several distinguished players, including David Garrick, Sybil Thorndike and Michael Redgrave, have over the centuries not regarded the part as beneath their dignity. The Chorus is an important figure in functional terms, as we have already seen, and his descriptive narrative could be delivered by means of a 'voice over' as far as its content goes, but what a loss it would be not to have a human presence before us, assuring us that there is nothing to be alarmed about in accomplishing such an immense imaginative leap as is proposed:

> There is the playhouse now, there must you sit,
> And thence to France shall we convey you safe
> And bring you back, charming the narrow seas
> To give you gentle pass; for, if we may,
> We'll not offend one stomach with our play.
>
> (Chorus to Act II, 36–40)

Indeed, in many respects he not only displays the cheerful confidence of many of Shakespeare's choric figures – compare, for example, Puck's buoyant tones in *A Midsummer Night's Dream* in forecasting that 'The man shall have his mare again, and all shall be well' – but he acts as a complementary image to that of Henry: his breezy reassurance that the feat of presenting Agincourt on stage can succeed is in direct parallel to Henry's bold belief that his faltering troops can storm the walls of Harfleur or that his 'island carrions' can overwhelm the vastly stronger French army. Like Henry, he has the common touch and wins the spectators' confidence as a man who knows what he is doing and yet makes light of it; remarks like the one about offending stomachs reveal a sense of the ridiculous, and by dint of such tactics he persuades us to accept his view of things and so conditions our response to the French expedition, the plight of the English troops and the legitimacy of Henry's claim. Indeed, it is through the Chorus's eyes that we most often view Henry; the phrases which are uppermost in our minds – 'the warlike Harry', 'the mirror of all Christian kings', 'The royal captain of this ruined band', 'A little touch of Harry in the night', 'This star of England' – are all of the Chorus's coinage, yet they would simply appear as mere publicity tags without the warm, confident personality of the speaker to give them context and an appropriate voice to animate them.

The action proper is set in train by the Archbishop and the Bishop of Ely, roles which are often either guyed in the modern theatre or ruthlessly cut. We shall need shortly to discuss their indispensability in terms of Shakespeare's theme, but for the present it may be as well to regard them as necessary presences. In them we see in large measure the functional aspect of Shakespearean characterization; indeed, it is often a failure to appreciate that function, and a desire to give the bishops 'character', that adds to the contemporary director's embarrassment when confronted with two figures whose job is to tell each other facts that they may be assumed to know already; for instance, what a reformed character Henry now is. To Canterbury is entrusted that histrionic quagmire, the 'Salic law speech', and here the Archbishop can scarcely be allowed to display 'personality' any more than a cabinet minister can in making some long statement to the House, or a barrister can in summing up for the prosecution. But elsewhere opportunities for bestowing human traits on both of the prelates are provided; there is a nice rueful touch of humour in the swift exchange which follows the revelation of just what the Church might lose if the Commons' bill were passed:

> ELY This would drink deep.
> CANTERBURY   'Twould drink the cup and all.

Even if we resist the temptation to visualize the ecclesiastics as scheming churchmen conversing in undertones and rubbing their hands at outwitting the irreligious Commons or at hoodwinking Henry by diverting his eyes towards France, the parts do not have to be merely cardboard cut-outs, like Olivier's film scenery. But we must also accept the element of 'scene-setting' contained in the roles.

A similar degree of dramatic necessity informs the parts of the English courtiers, and even the traitorous trio of Cambridge, Scroop and Grey are permitted little in the way of individual colouring. The personalities of the French court are far more interesting as human specimens, doubtless because Shakespeare is not under the same conceptual pressure to make the Frenchmen present a united front as he is with Henry's

Masterstudies: Henry V

Englishmen. Hence the opportunities for character clashes are there for the taking, and in the supercilious and acerbic Dauphin Shakespeare found the perfect irritant to accentuate the disagreements within the foreign ranks and to anticipate their undoing at the time of national crisis. The Dauphin's cocky underestimation of his foe's true mettle is made apparent even before he first appears on stage, and the same arrogant note colours his first speech (II. 4. 14–29). Even more relevant to his subsequent behaviour is his direct contradiction of the Constable of France when that worthy assures him that his assessment of Henry requires updating:

> Well, 'tis not so, my Lord High Constable;
> But though we think it so, it is no matter,
>
> (lines 41–2)

a speech of such condescension that it neatly paves the way to the bickering which forms the keynote to the pre-Agincourt scene in Act III (if we accept the Folio text's speech prefixes for this scene, and do not assign the Dauphin's lines to the Duke of Bourbon, as does the quarto version of the play).

The presence of the Dauphin through most of the action certainly helps to unify the French scenes, and the notion of a running feud between the Constable and the French prince provides an element of character contrast welcome in episodes where the other French noblemen seem virtually interchangeable. The Constable supplies a counterbalance to the figure of Exeter on the English side, though he is a far less monolithic presence. Unlike the Dauphin, he does not appear to be motivated by feelings of personal affront in opposing the English challenge; he does not underestimate Henry's new-found dignity, yet though he is at a loss to explain how the English climate can breed such fighting men, he believes a sight of the army opposed to him will force Henry to bid for terms (III. 5. 15–26, 55–60). But the finest chances for the actor playing the Constable come in Act III, Scene 7, where the scrapping with the Dauphin is renewed, with the additional foil of Orleans to enhance it. The contrasts are nicely drawn: the Dauphin, young, eager and idealistic, but foolishly arrogant; the Constable, less impetuous, more 'laid back', treating this as one more battle, humouring his prince and yet sufficiently exasperated by his extravagance to put him down; Orleans, neutral enough not to join in baiting the Dauphin, yet not defending him in his presence, content with rebuking the Constable for ignoring the good qualities of the man in one of the best prose rallies in the piece (III. 7. 90–121); Rambures, interjector of tactful questions intended no doubt to distract the Constable from his prey. Such skilful

Henry V

handling of this group of noble names is wonderfully entertaining at such a tense moment in the fortunes of Henry's army, but such flashes of personality are never rekindled in the battle scenes, and a promising resolution of the Dauphin–Constable rivalry is never forthcoming.

The only other French male worth more than a passing word is the herald, Montjoy, whose surname we never learn, 'Montjoy' being an official title, like 'Chester Herald' or 'Rouge Dragon'. This part would again appear to be a purely functional one, yet this dignified officer of the French crown often makes a striking impression on stage, as a man with a job of work to do who seems to win Henry's respect for that very reason. Montjoy's speech on his first entry in Act III, Scene 6 is curt and even insolent in tone:

> You know me by my habit.
>
> (line 111)

His message, as we have seen, is deliberately formalized and may even be regarded as humorously so, but his mode of speech appears to increase in deference when he returns in Act IV, Scene 3, as if (like those who encounter Tamburlaine in Marlowe's tragedy) he was impressed despite himself, and a genuine regret seems to inspire his parting statement.

> Thou never shalt hear herald any more.
>
> (line 127)

It is of course as a thoroughly abashed and saddened figure that he returns in Act IV, Scene 7 to crave leave to identify the dead; the semi-jocular addressing of Henry as 'King Harry' of IV.3 is now transformed into that of 'great king' (used twice). The impression is that even a mere functionary can be moved by the triumph and tragedy of experiencing military greatness at close quarters; Montjoy is, in old-fashioned parlance, 'a decent chap'.

But what of those of the English rank-and-file, who do not deserve such a phrase applied to them? Clearly the ordinary soldiery must provide much of the comedy in a military chronicle, and the two quartets – Bardolph, Nym, Pistol and the Boy; Fluellen, Gower, Macmorris and Jamy – contain some of the most colourful and boldly outlined personalities in the play. Yet they are none of them made out of Shakespeare's most original raw materials: they are caricatures rather than characters in the fullest sense, while the Boy plays little more than a functional or choric part in the action, though he contributes his reminiscences to the memorial sketch of Falstaff in Act II, Scene 3. His best moments come in his direct address to the audience in Act III, Scene 2, where he discourses on the inadequacies of the 'three swashers', in a

Masterstudies: **Henry V**

speech of striking stylistic dexterity, and again in Act IV, Scene 4, where he acts as translator to Pistol and M. Le Fer, and supplies a few lines of commentary on the fates of his former masters, Nym and Bardolph. There is a measure of fun to be extracted from the pseudo-belligerence of all three Eastcheap Irregulars, but it involves little exploration of character. The humour of the scenes in which they appear lies more in what they say than in what they are.

In the same way the quartet of officers, despite their national idiosyncrasies and regional accents, is not particularly remarkable, although Paul Jorgensen has been able to demonstrate just how carefully Shakespeare observed the gradations of military rank – as promulgated in contemporary textbooks of military conduct – in creating the portraits of the four captains, as well as those of Lieutenant Bardolph, Ancient Pistol and Corporal Nym. Even Macmorris's touchiness concerning his nationality has been shown to be based on actual incidents where Irish soldiers serving in the English army were similarly sensitive to suggestions that they came of alien stock.

Shakespeare is careful not to trot out *all* the hackneyed clichés touching on national characteristics in depicting his archetypes – Fluellen is not shown as a devotee of toasted cheese or the sound of the harp, for example – but otherwise there is only the liveliness of the dialogue to distinguish these portraits from similar ones elsewhere in our literature. Strenuous efforts usually have to be made in production to make anything much of Gower, the least caricatured figure of the group, although Gary Taylor's ingenious suggestion that the lines can be read as the utterances of a thickish 'chinless wonder' deserves to be put to the test of live performance. Macmorris is pugnacious and bloodthirsty, but little more; Jamy is disappointing, which leaves Fluellen, who is indisputably the main force for comedy in the play, in the absence of Falstaff. William Hazlitt found him 'the most entertaining character in the piece', and he is certainly permitted to achieve one of the minor victories of the play, when he forces his abominable leek down Pistol's throat, which compensates those with Celtic sensitivities for the way Henry leads him up the garden path over the glove in Williams's cap. Fluellen's pedantic insistence on the 'small print' touching on the conduct of battles is nicely undercut in these scenes, but to employ the phraseology of Corporal Nym, Fluellen's personality is too dominated by 'the humour of it', and he is limited to that very enjoyable but finite function, although his blind support for Henry has been taken by some modern critics as a mark of gullibility.

Hazlitt, who was entertained by Fluellen, professed to be outraged by Henry, and although a distaste for the historical figure may have con-

Henry V

ditioned his response, we cannot bypass his charge that Shakespeare's play glamorizes warfare and those who wage it. Part of Shakespeare's problem in creating a convincing persona for his hero was that the Elizabethan public had taken Henry to their hearts, and Elizabethan playwrights were largely obliged to follow suit, regardless of their own personal feelings on the subject. It cannot be stressed too often that we shall never know what 'the man Shakespeare' truly thought of Henry V. But, as was argued in the introduction, many commentators have felt unhappy with the suggestion that Shakespeare was prepared to present this English monarch as worthy of respect or even admiration, when his chief claim to fame seems to be that he led his army on a senseless quest for glory and conquest. Sufficient has been said in these pages by now, it is hoped, to set such objections in some kind of perspective.

But leaving aside Elizabethan expectations and authorial attitudes, a number of critics have expressed deep reservations about the character as it appears within the pages of the text; typical is W. B. Yeats who in 1901 contrasted Henry unfavourably with Richard II:

... having made the vessel of porcelain, Richard II, he had to make the vessel of clay, Henry V. He makes him the reverse of all that Richard was. He has the gross vices, the coarse nerves, of one who is to rule among violent people ... He is as remorseless and undistinguished as some natural force, and the finest thing in his play is the way his old companions fall out of it broken-hearted or on their way to the gallows ...

In a similar vein Mark Van Doren, in *Shakespeare* (1939), felt an obvious distaste for a creation which he believed had not stimulated the writer's imagination to the full:

Shakespeare has forgotten the glittering young god whom Vernon described in *Henry IV* – plumed like an estridge or like an eagle lately bathed, shining like an image in his golden coat ... The figure whom he has groomed to be the ideal English king, all plumes and smiles and decorated courage, collapses here into a mere good fellow, a hearty undergraduate with enormous initials on his chest. The reason is that Shakespeare has little interest in the ideal English king ... Henry is Shakespeare's last attempt at the great man who is also simple ...

A few years later, Una Ellis-Fermor in *The Frontiers of Drama* (1945) went further in diagnosing a deficiency in the royal character:

Henry V has indeed transformed himself into a public figure; the most forbidding thing about him is the completeness with which this has been done. He is solid and flawless. There is no attribute of him that is not part of this figure, no desire, no interest, no habit even that is not harmonized with it ... It is in vain that we look for the personality of Henry behind the king; there is nothing else there ... We see the diplomacy, the soldiership, the vigilant, astute eye upon the moods of

Masterstudies: Henry V

the people and barons, the excellent acting of a part in court and camp and council-room, and only when we try to look into the heart of the man do we find that it is hardly acting at all, that the character has been converted whole to the uses of the function, the individual utterly eliminated, sublimated, if you will. There is no Henry, only a king.

As we shall see later, a number of more recent critics have continued this line, some regarding the king as a morally culpable figure, hypocritical and self-righteous, others attributing his 'flat' character to the position in Shakespeare's historical sequence which *Henry V* occupies. M. M. Reese takes this line in *The Cease of Majesty* (1961) when he says:

After the sustained conflicts of the two preceding plays, *Henry V* is in the main a demonstration. The hero is no longer in the toils. The end has proved the man, and his victory over himself has been much more than a personal victory. Riot and dishonour have been put to flight, reason is passion's master, and England has at last a king who can physic all her ills . . . In *Henry V* Shakespeare celebrates England's recovered majesty through the deeds of 'the mirror of all Christian kings'.

Others have been even more charitable to the figure the playwright created; for H. A. Evans, who edited the first Arden edition in 1903, there was little doubt that:

Conscientious, brave, just, capable and tenacious, Henry stands before us the embodiment of worldly success, and as such he is entitled to our unreserved admiration . . .

For Charles Williams in 1936, the king before Agincourt is almost touched with divinity:

He 'loves' his present pains and his spirit is therefore eased. He has rather more than accepted darkness, danger, defeat, and death, and loves them. It is this which gives him a new quickening of the mind, new motions of the organs; it destroys sloth and the drowsy grave of usual life. It is this love and the resulting legerity of spirit which enable him to be what the Chorus describes . . . We are clean away from the solemn hero-king, and therefore much more aware of the Harry of the Chorus, and of the thing he is – the 'touch of Harry in the night' . . .

J. Dover Wilson, in his introduction to the New Cambridge edition of 1947, was inclined to believe that after the bloodless surrender of Harfleur,

. . . we have the first glimpse of a real man behind the traditional heroic mask. From this moment we are brought close and closer to him, until we come, if not to know him well, at least to do him homage, even to think of him with affection; the homage and affection some of us pay to a Nelson or a Gordon.

Henry V

To J. H. Walter, Henry's finest hour came on the night before the decisive action; to the Arden editor, his behaviour here was little short of impeccable:

> His courage is magnificent, and his extraordinary self-control has not always been acknowledged. He does not unpack his heart and curse like a drab, nor flutter Volscian dovecots, nor unseam his enemies from the nave to the chaps, he is no tragic warrior hero, he is the epic leader strong and serene, the architect of victory.

Without prolonging the selective quotations, it may be easily demonstrated what a wide variety of Henries there are to choose from: the super-hero whose qualities Shakespeare admired and endorsed; the magnificent commonplace whom Shakespeare felt duty-bound to present but whose epic stature proved unamenable to engrossing characterization; the Machiavellian tactician who manipulated others into taking responsibility for what he chose to do; the human being who immersed his more engaging traits in exercising his official authority; an astute and efficient leader with some appealing and some less laudable tendencies. Which interpretation comes closest to the Henry of Shakespeare's play? The only way forward is to examine the evidence supplied by the text.

The epic imagery of the Prologue reminds us immediately that Shakespeare's hands were tied in large measure when he came to characterize Henry: the king was a public icon for the Elizabethans, a 'warlike' monarch who epitomized successful military endeavour for a nation that still found validity in that concept. But it is significant that when the king is first discussed (and of course not all descriptions of off-stage heroes in Shakespeare are to be trusted, as Iago's portrait of Othello bears witness), he is not extolled for aggressive or martial qualities, but rather for his dedication, his piety, his 'grace and fair regard'. Canterbury, in his long encomium (I. 1. 38–59), urges both his erudition and his eloquence, the former providing some sort of a rebuttal to the charge, mounted by Yeats and other critics, that Henry is coarse-grained and no kind of an intellectual. If we wish to argue that Canterbury is here speaking in character rather than as a choric narrator, then his words may be held to be unctuously flattering to the king whom he hopes to divert from annexing church property, but there seems to be no justification for claiming that what he says is a tissue of lies. The accent on Henry's reformation should not obscure what kind of a paragon he has reformed himself into. Certainly, we are being prepared for the arrival of someone other than a militant thug.

Act I, Scene 2 is Henry's first test as far as those commentators antagonistic to him are concerned: they see him as either bamboozled by his archbishop into making war on France, or as himself tricking his archbishop into bolstering his own predatory urge to go to war, through legal manoeuvrings and religious platitudes. That the clerics have a vested interest in diverting Henry from their possessions is made clear, but we learn, even before France is mentioned, that the pious king is more inclined to support the Church than its despoilers (I. 1. 71–4), and the fact that he entrusts the archbishop with the task of expounding Henry's claim may be more an acknowledgement that in the Middle Ages ecclesiastics were more often than not pillars of the state as well, than an attempt to depict Canterbury as a wily *éminence grise*, with Henry as his stooge. The cleric's role here must not be too personalized: his exposition of Salic law is not an opportunity for some telling character acting.

Henry's own demeanour in this scene is vital: although some accuse him of hypocrisy, others assume him to be serious in his urgent questionings of the archbishop as to the rightness (and righteousness) of the claim he is making. We may not like what he is proposing to do, but surely Shakespeare depicts him as sincere in the way he goes about finding out if he ought to do it or not? His evident Christian conviction (already established by report) is everywhere apparent as he asks the prelate to unfold 'justly and religiously' the relevance of the Salic law to his own firmly held belief that he has a right to rule over France. To us Henry's obsessive quest for a second crown may seem absurdly misguided; we do not see it as a sacred and inescapable duty for the king to wrest France from those keeping it from him, once his right is proved absolute. But to his contemporaries and to their Elizabethan successors (some of whom would after all have remembered a time when England possessed Calais), Henry's task was doubtless plainly perceived: the only point at issue was whether or not the claim could be justified.

Much has been made of the tedium of Canterbury's Salic law speech; even Dover Wilson admitted that the speech puzzled him:

Why did Shakespeare, generally ready to sacrifice almost anything in his sources likely to induce boredom in the audience, transplant therefrom this tiresome genealogical lecture, sixty-three lines long, and full of obscure names, some of which he did not even trouble to transcribe correctly?

The usual argument is that the Elizabethans would have expected to hear something of the kind, would indeed have been genuinely interested in it, but more likely (in my view) is the fact that a theatre audience needs to know that *Henry* treats his claim responsibly. Without the speech and its 'tedium', we should lack the reassurances that Shakespeare

Henry V

is at pains to see we receive. It is ironic that the king, often painted as a troublemaking, aggressive 'toughie', is in fact depicted as a man of conscience, a term he couples with 'right' when questioning the archbishop as to the moral validity of what he is planning to do. Whatever his motives for involving the Church, surely Henry at least convinces us that he will not be waging war lightly or without the best support he can obtain?

Nor is he reckless in mobilizing his troops: in the theatre, little or nothing is usually made of Henry's circumspection in defending the Scottish border, a detail unlikely to have been lost on an audience watching the play in 1599, only a dozen years or so after the execution of Mary Queen of Scots. Henry's reception of the French embassy is equally cool and wary, and his treatment of the ambassadors, even after the Dauphin's gift, reminds us that this man was renowned for his merciful demeanour in comparison with many contemporary rulers. The lines in which he responds to the Dauphin's present do offer some cue for anger, but Henry's passion is leavened with touches of wit, and though his indignation perhaps smacks too much of self-congratulatory self-righteousness to us, we have to bear in mind that monarchs on stage are often required to speak the language of their office, rather than in their own persons. Once again, the concept of Shakespearean lines as revelatory of character may have to be abandoned when a figure is speaking a commentary on his or her own intentions or achievements; it is often the only available means at the author's disposal to convey information or to create the appropriate dramatic atmosphere. Though some critics have stressed it, personal pique is only one factor in Henry's address to the ambassadors. And the same proviso applies to his attitude towards the traitor lords in Act II, Scene 2. His reputation for mercy enhanced by his clemency towards the drunken soldier, Henry is then able to expose the unforgiving mentalities of those who are ostensibly concerned for his wellbeing and security: some critics have disliked this piece of trickery on Henry's part, but it is perhaps his privilege as potential victim of these underhand conspirators to turn the tables on them, and he is surely no more culpable than Christ when he tricked those who sought to stone the woman taken in adultery, by suggesting the least sinful accuser took first throw?

The long speech on treason has already been discussed in the section on language, but its relevance to the building-up of the character portrait of Henry is in my view negligible: it does not stand as a personal utterance by a psychological type so much as a set-piece on a familiar topic of the day. Henry is no more revealing his individual temperament here than he is when he passes sentence. More 'characterful' is the cheerful

Masterstudies: Henry V

observation that the discovery of the conspiracy represents a good omen, followed by the entrusting of the English cause to God. To some this will be a matter of repugnance, but the concept of a 'God of battles' is not entirely defunct even today.

We have then, I suggest, in the initial presentation of Henry, an attempt to create a favourable impression of the monarch as national leader, which is not to say that Henry has to be regarded as either an interesting or complex personality or a perfect human specimen. At this stage it is true that (as Thomas Kenny observed in 1864) the king is shown to be 'a complete, harmonious, self-possessed character' but also true that 'such characters are not dramatic', because we never see him 'caught in the struggle of passions which we know to be but distant and latent elements in our own nature'. What come across most memorably in the first two acts of the piece are Henry's seriousness, his devotion to his duties, his religious faith; admirable qualities and, in my opinion (though not that of others), these qualities are untainted by hypocrisy or deceit, although for me they are not inseparable from the faintest traces of priggishness. Henry in Acts I and II is, if dull, still a figure to be admired, if grudgingly; can it be claimed that he continues in this vein?

He is next seen urging his troops into the breach in Harfleur's defences, and once again a number of critics have seen the private man submerged in the public figure to Henry's detriment: his concerns are less for the feelings of his soldiers as individuals than for the morale of his army as a whole. But what war leader in any age has been able to command a fighting force and get the best out of it, while still treating each man as an isolated unit? Henry does in fact demonstrate in this famous speech a good deal of psychological understanding of the forces under him: he does not denigrate the peacetime virtues of 'modest stillness and humility', but he emphasizes that an effort of conscious will is now needed to transform these laudable attributes into aggression, following this with an appeal to the English proneness to ancestor worship. He does not – as Jorgensen claims – discriminate between 'you noblest English' and the 'men of grosser blood'; to Henry all his troops are equal partners, a line to which he will return just before the decisive battle:

> For there is none of you so mean and base
> That hath not noble lustre in your eyes.
>
> (III. 1. 29–30)

If wars are to inspire notable oratory, we might be hard pressed to find a more effective example of it than this, though some regard the lines as strained and forced. And of course it is precisely Henry's *effectiveness* that some people cannot forgive Shakespeare for.

Henry V

Many more cannot bring themselves to condone Henry's threatening words before the walls of Harfleur in Act III, Scene 3: the ghastly images of war as it affects innocent civilians are nowhere more feelingly conjured up in Shakespeare's works, and some suspicion has been expressed that Henry is again 'passing the buck' here, and justifying his own insatiable desire for slaughter and conquest by informing the townsfolk that it will be on their own heads if his forces are unleashed on the defenceless people. The suggestion that Henry is unable to control his ravening hordes is of course something his opponents have seized on as a further illustration of his tendency to blame others for his own actions, but given Henry's reputation as a disciplinarian, is it possible that Shakespeare knew that spectators would easily recognize the dimension of bluff in the sovereign's words? It has at any rate been conclusively demonstrated by J. H. Walter and others that Henry's efforts to frighten the citizens of Harfleur into capitulation by using dire threats were entirely in accordance with current military theory and practice.

But it is notable that a figure of more human tendencies does begin to emerge from this point on; despite the chilling pronouncement on the penalties for looting, Henry's encounter with Fluellen in Act III, Scene 6, prefaced as it is with the striking Folio stage-direction: 'Enter the King and his poore Souldiers', helps to deprive this paragon of some of his remoteness – he even addresses Fluellen with the more egalitarian 'you' at line 99 – and his order that the native population is to be treated with courtesy is echoed by his compliment to Montjoy that he executes his duties efficiently. Moreover, his frank admission that his forces are depleted through sickness takes off any hint of arrogance from his reply to Montjoy's suggestion that he should seek ransom. If we are inclined to wish Bardolph's life had been spared, the allusions to the desperate plight of Henry and his men help to explain, if not completely vindicate, the absolute strictness of the king's decree.

The jovially moralistic tone of Henry's opening lines in Act IV, Scene 1 can sound horribly false, but Shakespeare must have found it difficult to demonstrate the king's 'cheerful semblance' by any other means, until the encounters in disguise later in the scene. The quick verbal scrap with Pistol is a mere preliminary to the central discussion with Bates, Court and Williams, which for many is the crux of the whole play. Henry (like the disguised Duke in *Measure for Measure*) is confronted with a few home truths concerning the way others view him, and it is clear that in seeking to prompt his hearers to a declaration of faith in the king's loyalty to his troops and in the justice of his cause, Henry receives far from reassuring responses. Yet in his soldiers' presence his words betray no sense of disappointment or affront, and that Henry is shown to be

Masterstudies: Henry V

chastened by the experience of mingling with his men may be doubted from the amusement he derives from setting up the practical joke with Williams's glove.

Where many commentators cease to admire Henry is in his evasive answer to Williams's perfectly justifiable query as to the fate of the common soldier slain in a conflict which for all he knows may be unjustified. The implied question, as Raymond Powell points out in *Shakespeare and the Critics' Debate* (1980), is whether even a just war can be reconciled with 'its inevitable cost in human terms'. Powell argues that Henry shifts the ground from the broadly human issue to the narrowly theological one of the king's lack of responsibility for the souls of the sinful who die in battle, and to Henry's detractors this is in keeping with the hypocrisy they are all too ready to lay at the king's door. All one can say is that Shakespeare was perhaps over-anxious to show Henry 'keeping his end up' when morale was flagging.

It is only when the soldiers have departed that Henry drops his guard and allows us to see a little of the man beneath the mask: diplomat, strategist, warrior, leader by turns, Henry now complains of the high price monarchy exacts from those born to wear a crown. Yet even here there is a coldly formal quality about the lines, as we have already noted; they do not really bear Henry's personal insignia; the sufferings cited are generalized, rather than specific, and reveal some contempt for the common man, rather than sympathy. In fact, there is a greater sense of individual utterance in the short speech which follows Erpingham's brief intrusion; through lines 282–98 there runs a convincingly particularized series of doubts and fears. The note of confidence is temporarily gone; the rhetoric is laid aside; the king, like the mangled dead invoked by Williams, has matters on his conscience too, and it is this admission of fallibility more than anything else which lets us realize, perhaps for the first time in the course of the drama, that Henry is a vulnerable man with frailties to confess and a mind haunted lest past crimes remain unexpiated. The mood passes, but in a sudden flash we receive an image of a tormented conscience behind the confident façade which can reconcile us to this apparent monolith with no secrets to hide. It is almost as if Henry, like Hamlet, whose history may already have been occupying Shakespeare's attention, has to abandon his splendid isolation and acknowledge the dirt on his hands before we can take him to our hearts. Moreover, his mental agony, however brief, makes his later inspirational behaviour that much more worthy of our admiration; he is not a man without doubts, but rather a man who has them under control. But they are there, and when he goes on in Act IV, Scene 3 to speak of himself and the English army as a band of brothers he is not patronizing them;

Henry V

he is declaring himself one of them by virtue of his own guilt and insecurity; he no more enjoys true peace of mind than the rest of his forlorn company.

In this context his 'Crispin's day' speech in IV. 3 assumes a high degree of significance; it is vital to grasp that Henry begins by cheering Westmorland in his despondency, and proclaiming that he only wishes to lead into battle those who wish to be there. He is working on his men's morale by suggesting to them that they form an élite who have something in common, ostensibly a desire for honour, but in fact, as we have seen, a shared humanity compounded of a mixture of tremulous hope and menacing terror. Henry's force has by now become identified with him in a way which was not even manifest before Harfleur, and there is a sense abroad of unity engendered by misfortune and wretchedness, which Henry proceeds to convert to optimism and self-confidence, as the lines given to Westmorland immediately following Henry's oration make clear. It will have been a privilege to serve under 'Harry the King' at Agincourt, and he paints a refreshingly humorous picture of the garrulous old men before the alehouse fire, feasting their neighbours every 24 October, and showing off their war-wounds with pride; they may even exaggerate a little:

> ... he'll remember, with advantages,
> What feats he did that day.
>
> (lines 50–1)

Such an honour will it prove to have been at Agincourt that 'gentlemen in England now abed' will curse their indolence that did not lead them to enrol in Henry's victorious army, and so participate in a share of its glory. Deprived of its rotten elements – its Cambridges, Scroops and Greys, its Nyms and its Bardolphs – Henry's force has indeed been whittled down to a 'band of brothers', and its majestic leader treats it as such. It is not easy to sustain a verdict of cold self-righteousness at this point, or suggest that rigid, impersonal efficiency has been achieved at the expense of human warmth. It is possible to *read* the 'Crispin's day' speech as another exercise in effective public relations, but to hear it *spoken* on stage by a charismatic actor, can one seriously believe that Shakespeare saw it being played tongue-in-cheek?

There are perhaps two further aspects of Henry's character to be fitted into the picture: one is his controversial decision in Act IV, Scene 6 to give the order for the slaughter of the French prisoners, which has been variously censured and defended. As Taylor's edition makes clear, it seems certain that part of this brutal action was carried out before the audience's eyes, or why should the Folio stage-direction for IV. 6 insist,

Masterstudies: Henry V

'Enter the King and his trayne, with Prisoners'? The English action certainly is explicable in the setting of Henry's perilous position in the battle, outnumbered as he is, and in the light of contemporary military theory and practice it can be explained away. But it is plain that what all the defensive arguments ignore is that Shakespeare was under no obligation to include this particular incident at all, especially in so bald a fashion, unless he had some good reason for doing so. The excuse sometimes given is that Henry's decision is a response to the massacre of the boys guarding the luggage, but if this were so, why did the dramatist not place Gower's reporting of that incident *before* the order to kill the prisoners? In fact, Gower is misinformed when he links the two events: Henry does not know of the attack on the baggage-train when he commands his troops to cut the French throats. There is a general feeling that Henry's order needs justification, and the play as we have it does not really supply the answer. Taylor makes a good deal of the incident, followed as it is by Fluellen's reminder to the audience that the king also had a hand in the destruction of Falstaff, a worse crime in some ways than Alexander's drunken murder of Cleitus.

All one can add is that there are signs of possible carelessness in the handling of the incident; in Act IV, Scene 6, the order is certainly given, and there are prisoners on stage if the action needs to be carried out in full view. In the following scene Gower says that the murders have now taken place (lines 8–10), but later Henry, entering in the company of 'Bourbon and prisoners', angered by the sight of the French refusing to fight, threatens that if they do not,

> ... we'll cut the throats of those we have.
>
> (line 61)

Are we to assume that the original threat was *not* carried out? Are we dealing with a separate group of prisoners in this scene? All is confused. If the slaughter of prisoners on stage could be established without doubt, then it might be interpreted as a further instance of Henry's identification with his common soldiery, his kingly escutcheon dented by another human blemish. But it might also be seen as an action of such necessity that no common soldier could bring himself to condemn it.

The grimness of battle is replaced by practical joking, as the diversion created by the king's jest with Fluellen and Williams supersedes the tumult of war; although we never read much of the actual fighting, no doubt on the Elizabethan stage there were plenty of physical skirmishes interwoven with the lines of the text, and the relief from tension provided by the king's recreation would not have been grudged him. Again, there is a sense of comradeship and good humour here, and it may once more

Henry V

be said to reinforce the picture of a leader who knows when to relax and enjoy the company of his social inferiors, not irresponsibly but in a spirit of genuine equality.

Many find the Henry of the final act difficult to accept, feeling his brash courtship of Katharine to be embarrassingly slick, even crudely offensive. But the conclusion of the action had to be comedic, and since courting and marriage were traditional emblems of communal reconciliation and harmony, it is hard to see how Shakespeare could have avoided the wooing scene, even without the example of *The Famous Victories* as precedent. Those who find Henry hypocritical as a statesman find him equally so as a wooer; others find his approach and attitude coarse and insensitive. Certainly, as Charles Gildon noted as early as 1714, Katharine's broken English is quite absurd in a French court where everyone else speaks the language perfectly, but her part in the dénouement is not negligible, and she sustains the female part in the duologue with spirit and individuality. The sexual badinage (later taken much further by Burgundy and the king), if not to modern taste, is a healthy acknowledgement of what is tacitly accepted, that this royal couple will be expected to breed and provide the joint kingdom with an heir apparent. If Henry is once again to be accused of playing a role, then he plays it with style and wit, and despite his protestations that he has no pretensions as a lover and that Kate must take him as he is, we know from other Shakespearean lovers that it is not always the smooth talkers whose sincerity is to be relied upon. It may also be another indication of Henry's new-won humanity and flexibility that he conducts his courtship in prose rather than verse, and uses homely imagery to impress his honest intentions on his intended bride. In the kind of society where his French counterpart writes sonnets to his horse, it is perhaps a good omen that Henry professes himself the plain-dealing soldier, however out of character it may appear to be to those who demand strict consistency in such matters.

If we attempt to sum up Henry's personality, there is no doubt that we shall soon become aware of many more such inconsistencies but, as I have stressed, it is misguided to look for the kind of coherence from the heroes and heroines of Renaissance drama that we expect to find in the pages of George Eliot or Henry James. And again, characters can often assume more unity and cohesion when presented by a performer on stage than they do when analysed 'cold' on the printed page. Henry can seem a mass of contradictions and yet galvanize us in the theatre, which is not to say that our reaction to him needs to be universally favourable or totally antipathetic. Much will depend on what we conceive to be the theme of the drama that bears his name.

Masterstudies: Henry V

Themes

Had this study of *Henry V* been called for even forty years ago, a discussion of its themes might have begun with Noël Coward's words spoken after the first night of *Cavalcade* in October 1931:

I hope this play has made you feel that, in spite of the troublous times we are living in, it is still pretty exciting to be English.

The fact that it would be virtually impossible to speak those words without irony from any stage in the world in the 1980s indicates just how hard it now is to persuade today's public that *Henry V* is nothing more than a popular piece of national propaganda for Elizabethan consumption. 'Shakespeare must have had some other purpose in mind' is the frequent assumption underlying the present-day reluctance to take the drama at face-value, as a straightforward treatment of the major achievement of a famous English monarch. To the play's original audiences it *was* 'pretty exciting' to be English, although they might not have phrased the matter so tamely; to a more self-consciously unchauvinistic age, *Henry V* must be rescued if possible from any taint of patriotic self-glorification.

One of the problems, therefore, in discussing the play's themes is that they may not always translate successfully into late twentieth-century terms. Much early commentary on the work assumed a patriotic slant, and we have to acknowledge the presence of nationalistic elements in the piece, whether we deplore their existence or not. What it is vital to grasp is that their contribution does not necessarily make the play any better or any worse as drama, a point which, had it been accepted a century ago, might have enabled us to obtain a clearer view of *Henry V* as a work of art that much sooner.

Furthermore, we happen to live in an age when complexity and ambiguity are still fashionable aesthetic criteria, so that the exclusive function of art is too often regarded as the reconciliation of opposing tendencies or the revelation of tensions and ironies within a seemingly cohesive structure. Confronted with *Henry V*, perhaps too many commentators feel obliged to discover hidden dichotomies, arcane paradoxes, secret ambivalences, beneath its apparently translucent surface, and so salvage the play's critical respectability. Because Shakespeare's plays in general achieve such depths of profundity, touch on so many of the contradictions and complications of the human condition and personal relationships, we are in danger of assuming that in everything he wrote there must be an ulterior meaning, a more shadowy significance than that which meets the eye. In setting out to determine the themes of *Henry V*, we have to exercise caution that we are not

Henry V

imposing a false complexity or straining after ambiguities in the text which spring from nothing more tangible than the desire to find them there. We must take care that what we claim to have discovered in the play does not arise from a sense of disappointment at what is actually present.

It is inevitable that a large majority of critics have located the play's central theme in the development of the personality and function of Henry himself, frequently incorporating into the discussion the portrait of Prince Hal as set forth in the two parts of *Henry IV*. Clearly, to the Elizabethans history was a matter of the impact of human personality on political events rather than of the influence of social and economic forces on human communities, and the titles of the majority of Elizabethan chronicle plays reflect this predisposition to view historical periods in terms of the temperaments of reigning monarchs. The standard method of characterizing Henry's reign has already been sketched in these pages: the irresponsible youth, the reformation of character upon accession, the ardent claim to the French throne, the military success, the achievement of the heart's desire, the premature death. To this Shakespeare added Hal's awareness of his own libertinage, which invested the sowing of wild oats with an air of calculation; he supplied the charismatic figure of Falstaff, whose companionable rascality cast an equivocal light on Henry's rejection of him and his subsequent death; he seems to have been at pains to present his hero as favourably as possible thereafter, increasing the perfection of his military conduct, preserving from Hall and Holinshed those deeds and utterances which exemplified the warrior-prince and suppressing many, though not all, of those factors which might diminish him in the eyes of an Elizabethan audience. Yet the playwright also seems to have been concerned to make his paragon not merely sympathetic but likeable, a cheery and comradely sort of commander who acknowledged his affinity with his troops by sharing not merely the physical danger but also the moral risks occasioned by war.

Thus it is that a significant number of commentators have regarded the play as a study in heroic achievement, as an exemplification of what Shakespeare's contemporaries valued in a monarch who could both lead and identify with his people. Because *Henry* was looked on as an idealized portrait of kingship rather than a realistic analysis, it was accepted that the picture would of necessity lack verisimilitude in the form of idiosyncratic touches of personality. Minor fallibilities, faults and foibles notwithstanding, Henry was not to be taken as a living, breathing human being, but rather as a symbol of royal virtue, somewhat like a king in some Byzantine mosaic. Shakespeare's motive for this was conceived to

Masterstudies: Henry V

be in keeping with his epic theme: dramatic tension was not to be achieved by means of conflicts within the central character; *Hamlet* was still to come.

But from Henry's relative 'flatness' of presentation other critics have drawn rather different conclusions, as we have already noted. Una Ellis-Fermor sets the tone in *The Frontiers of Drama* when she says, 'There is no Henry, only a king.' One of those who has taken this argument to fruitful lengths is Derek Traversi, who sees the youthful Hal at first tainted by contact with those vicious and anarchic elements associated with Bolingbroke's usurpation of the throne: the young prince has to familiarize himself with the seamier aspects of his future kingdom before he is fit to rule it. When he finally assumes his royal office, he is obliged to repudiate his former cronies as emblems of that disorder he has pledged himself to eradicate both in himself and in the nation at large. As Traversi expresses the matter in *Shakespeare from Richard II to Henry V* (1957):

That rejection is, from the point of view of his growth as a public figure, the necessary external consequence of his acceptance of his royal vocation; this requires a visible turning away from the 'misrule' which is the supreme enemy of true kingship, and without it his later triumphs would be inconceivable. In *Henry V*, the king, having finally and with complete self-consciousness assumed the barely human responsibilities of his office, is at last able to use the knowledge he has gained of men and affairs to lead a nation from which the figure of 'riot' has been finally expelled to his victorious enterprise in France.

But, as Traversi argues, there is a price to be paid for success, and for this critic it involves a loss of compassion, a quality which Falstaff's erstwhile presence has underlined; the political abilities needed to recall a nation to a sense of its own destiny must be offset by a stance of indifference towards those wayward individuals who compose its population. For Traversi, Henry is far from flawless as a human specimen: the king has to exercise iron self-control in his political capacity, but violent passion cannot always be kept below the surface. Henry's assumption of his kingly function is often betrayed by his more fallible self which has the effect at times of calling his authority in question:

... it would be wrong to suppose that Shakespeare, in portraying Henry, intends to stress a note of hypocrisy. His purpose is rather to bring out certain contradictions, human and moral, which seem to be inherent in the notion of a successful king. As the play proceeds, Henry seems increasingly to be, at least in the moral sense, the victim of his position ... The administration of justice, upon which depends order within the kingdom and success in its foreign wars, demands from the monarch an impersonality which borders on the inhuman.

An Approach to Shakespeare (1956)

Henry V

The theme of the play, thus conceived (and Traversi's diagnosis does not seek to account for what many regard as Henry's sparks of humanity), turns out to be the potentially tragic one in which the human capacity for right conduct and true judgement is achieved at the expense of impulse and instinct, traits which we suppress at immense risk to our psyche. For Traversi, Henry's ruthless self-control is only attained through the loss of his finer and more attractive qualities; political necessity not only dictates the rejection of Falstaff but the annihilation of Prince Hal.

Many other critics have found Henry less than amiable, for all his breeziness as a wooer and his sense of camaraderie as a warrior, and are less prepared than Traversi to attribute his faults to the pressures of office. We have already noted the adverse comments of W. B. Yeats and Mark Van Doren and, more recently, others have added to their picture of the footballing hearty with gross tastes and crude sentiments, a more sinister dimension involving deceit and duplicity. It is significant that hard on the heels of the horrors of World War I Gerald Gould, in 'A New Reading of *Henry V*', published in the *English Review* in 1919, should argue that Shakespeare 'must have felt revolted by Henry's brutal and degrading "militarism"'. But more recent commentators have been less repelled by this tendency than by what they see as Henry's hypocrisy in persuading the Church to bolster the legitimacy of his claim to the French throne with spurious arguments of dubious validity, of cloaking his aggressive designs with a veneer of pious righteousness, of trading on the Archbishop's desire to divert secular eyes from sacred property, of breaking Falstaff's heart and dispatching his followers, of merely adopting a pose as the common soldiers' best friend, of evading Williams's implied question as to whether or not the war with France is justified and so forth. Moreover, those who might be reluctant to press *all* these charges are still united in their concern that Henry is regularly portrayed as unwilling to assume responsibility for actions he has decided to carry out, and as anxious to pin any blame thus incurred on others, be it the Archbishop of Canterbury, the Dauphin, the conspirators whose advice he turns against themselves at Southampton or even the common soldiers who die in battle with sins on their consciences.

This mode of interpretation has led several critics to engage in strongly worded attacks on Henry's nature, none more vehement than Harold C. Goddard's in his book *The Meaning of Shakespeare* (1951), where the king is dismissed as 'a coarse and brutal highway robber'. In the ensuing thirty-five years, an increasingly audible and influential body of opinion has sprung up, dedicated to the notion that in *Henry V* Shakespeare set out to expose the Machiavellian side of the great national hero, and

Masterstudies: **Henry V**

subtly to undercut the heroics epitomized by, and the noble sentiments expressed in, the person of the leader of his people, by inserting indications of his ruthlessness, brutality and duplicity at appropriate intervals. As early as 1961, M. M. Reese in *The Cease of Majesty* expressed his astonishment 'at the prejudice Henry has managed to arouse. In all the canon only Isabella, in *Measure for Measure*, has stirred so much personal distaste', and the adverse opinions have by no means decreased in severity since that date. One of the more judicious of the detractors, Zdenek Stribrny, sums up the essence of the case mounted by Henry's opponents:

However fervently Henry's ideal qualities are hammered home, they represent only half the poet's whole truth about the King and his holy war. A deeper analysis, probing under the shining surface, will find that the highlights in Henry's portrait are thrown into relief by dark shades

Stribrny goes on to indict Henry on the familiar charges of passing the buck, 'of hiding the bad conscience of an aggressor under constant references to God', of behaving badly to Katharine and contemptuously towards his soldiers before Agincourt. Stribrny's conclusion is closely akin to that of Traversi:

to less idealistic interpreters Henry reveals a less comforting but perhaps more rewarding dramatic character of a conquering king who has to pay a heavy human toll for his success. His good qualities are seen as reaching their richest and most interesting point by being both contrasted with, and dynamized by, equally potent qualities of the opposite tendency.

Others have been less charitable; C. H. Hobday in *Shakespeare Survey* 21 (1970) deduced from a study of the play's imagery that 'whatever Shakespeare may say about Henry, in his heart he regarded him as a murderer', and saw in the whole piece a sustained irony which undermined the 'fine talk of honour and religion with the realities of human greed and cruelty'. Hobday is inclined to doubt the word of 'two Popish prelates' set before a Protestant London audience when they extol Henry's Christian virtues, seeing Henry as accepting what amounts to a bribe from the archbishop in order to protect the Church's lands. The claim to the French crown, the justification for the war, the negligible nature of Henry's personal contribution to the English victory are all stressed, and the play is treated as an expression of the war-weary spirit of 1599: 'It would be surprising if Shakespeare had not been affected by the widespread anti-war feeling.' Hobday's explanation of the non-appearance of Falstaff in the piece is that his continued presence at

Henry's side might have turned the play into an anti-war satire: 'with Sir John in it, *Henry V* might have done for the Hundred Years' War what *Troilus and Cressida* did for the Trojan war...'

In the *Journal of the History of Ideas* for January–March 1976, Gordon Ross Smith goes further than Hobday, seeing the play as an exposé of the shallow kind of patriotism which is so often invoked on occasions of great national tension, attributing to the king other motives for his actions than those he proclaims so freely:

Henry gallops apace on his fiery-footed war-horse, waves the flag, emulates the voice of Stentor, and summons his countrymen to march his way in well-beseeming ranks. But the spectator who retains his own judgment knows that Henry wages war to busy giddy minds with foreign quarrels, that he does so to waste the memory of his father's usurpation, that he jails and forgets the legitimate heir [the Earl of March], that he executes his domestic enemies who would advance the heir, that he professedly executes them not out of malice but for reasons of state, and that in secret he knows all these things are wrong... These observations are not to deny the many and obvious merits of Henry V but only to insist that the grave and central faults of his position are obscured but not obliterated by all that technicolored patriotism..

Smith's analysis has the virtue of giving *Henry V* the kind of topicality and universality other critics have denied it, but he is perhaps in too much danger of creating a Shakespeare made in the image of the modern pacifist.

One other essay denigrating the play deserves respectful attention; appearing in *Shakespeare Survey* 30 (1977), along with William Babula's 'Whatever Happened to Prince Hal?' Andrew Gurr's '*Henry V* and the Bees' Commonwealth' treats the play as a sustained examination of the justification for Henry's war with France, and of the king's insecurity on a throne to which he recognizes that his title is dubious. Gurr sees Henry as motivated by a desire for personal glory and a secure title to his crown, and extracts from several relevant sixteenth-century works contemporary opinions which can be made to shed a dubious light on the morality of Henry's conduct. Gurr pays particular attention to the order to slaughter the French prisoners in Act IV, Scene 6, demonstrating that Elizabethan sentiment was divided as to its justification, but that Shakespeare chose the least favourable version of the incident for inclusion in his text, a factor which combined with the 'wrongheaded good will' with which Gower and Fluellen react to the command suggests that we should set aside the traditional concept of Henry as the ideal warrior-prince and view him rather as a hardheaded pragmatist whose reputation for clemency is undeserved:

Masterstudies: Henry V

The king, under supreme pressure, takes personal responsibility for the monstrosities of war which he is so keenly aware of. For the sake of victory he sets aside lenity and takes so many deaths on his conscience. In victory he is an Alexander, at least to Fluellen, and in victory we should perhaps overlook the fact that Augustine condemned Alexander as an unjust warrior. Lenity stops at the national boundary. Its upholder will bear the responsibility for foreign slaughter if slaughter can secure it the goodwill of homebred spirits.

Like several other earlier critics, Gurr sees significance in the fact that apparently the only actual combat set forth on stage is the squalid skirmish between Pistol and M. Le Fer in Act IV, Scene 4, a comic encounter which nonetheless exposes Pistol's base motives for going to war at all. Although the scene partly exists (for Gurr at least) to undercut the heroics of the Chorus, it also has a grimmer aspect, reinforcing the theme of self-interest (rather than that of the dispassionate search for honour or right) which this astute commentator sees running like a thread through the action. Even then, self-interest is not to be exclusively condemned; its presence may undermine the heroic dimension in the play, but *Henry V* demonstrates how it can be employed to unite a nation behind a popular if fallible leader.

In recent years, then, it has become increasingly common to see the play's theme in terms of human inadequacies, personal self-deception, political manipulation and the modern revulsion from the image of war as a glorious and inspirational phenomenon. Far from being read as a study in idealized monarchy, *Henry V* for many is now taken as an essay in *realpolitik*, an exposé of sovereignty in action and the hollowness of the notion of 'a glorious victory'. Far from being an admiring exploration of a great national figure, Shakespeare's play has recently begun to be treated as an expression of *fin-de-siècle* disillusionment with the values Henry appears to uphold, a reflection of national disenchantment with war and politicians, a piece of anti-heroic propaganda. Shakespeare, it is argued, was too fine a spirit, too sensitive a character, not to be aware of Henry's weaknesses and defects of personality, and to make them the true theme of his play.

That Henry is not the simple symbol of kingly perfection that earlier readers and spectators once saw can scarcely be denied: Shakespeare's creations are all myriad-faceted phenomena, and even if he strove to eliminate chronicle material detrimental to the king, he is unable as an artist to endow Henry with purely positive qualities. That the king is more complex than appears at first sight, we may readily grant. But that we can proceed from this admission to reconstruct the play as an adverse or even a critical portrait of an unscrupulous, ruthless, devious or merely fallible English sovereign is almost certainly to mistake warts and blem-

Henry V

ishes for the complexion as a whole. Or so it seems to the present writer. Despite the possibly equivocal motives of the clerics and Henry's own propensity to involve others in responsibility for his own decisions; despite the presumed callousness of his treatment of his erstwhile companions and his insistence on a loyalty to his person which some might feel to be misplaced in view of his own dubious claim to the crown; despite his martial rhetoric, his threatening words and the evasive response to the worried enquiries of his men on the eve of Agincourt; despite his order to dispatch the French prisoners and his treatment of Katharine as one of the spoils of war; can it be truly maintained that our awareness of these flaws and errors *outweighs* the impression that we receive of Henry's more commendable qualities? What we conceive to be the theme of the drama must largely depend on the degree of importance which we attach to the less attractive elements in Shakespeare's presentation of his hero, and whether we regard them as a vital or an incidental part of his design.

Certainly there remains a substantial body of opinion dedicated to the notion that in *Henry V* Shakespeare retained an image of kingship which, although far from uncritically conceived, still upheld the historical and dramatic tradition of Henry's general excellence. Inevitably such an assertion does not always manifest the dynamism and excitement evident in more iconoclastic interpretations, but it does offer a corrective to attempts to give undue weight to the sometimes anachronistic concept of a badly discredited Henry. Robert Ornstein in *The Cease of Majesty*, by no means unaware of Henry's shortcomings and willing to admit that the royal ideals are far from being absolute, especially when viewed in a late twentieth-century light, nevertheless believes that for Shakespeare his king was endearing not because of his regal achievements but because he shares our humanity:

where *Henry V* celebrates the victory of the English Caesar, *Antony and Cleopatra* suggests that 'tis paltry to be Caesar. But we do not thrill in *Henry V* to the fulfillment of Harry's ambition to be sole sir of England and France. What we rejoice in is the small time of brotherhood which Harry and his soldiers share at Agincourt; and what redeems the warlike Harry are precisely those human needs which we cannot imagine in the coldblooded Octavius: the anguish of conscience and the loneliness that prompts him to confess his fears and to seek the companionship of his men around the campfire ...

Far from proving to be a historical drama with ironic, even tragic overtones, *Henry V* by such an analysis proves to possess a regenerative dimension, and a number of recent critics have preferred to treat the play in this way, emphasizing that (as in comedy) harmony and success

Masterstudies: Henry V

emerge only after the hero has undergone a prolonged period of stress and self-discovery. Such an assessment certainly helps to explain and justify the final act of the drama which has been found both incongruous and disappointing by generations of critics, but which comes into its own if we see it as the culmination of a romantic success story, in which the hero, having passed through countless vicissitudes, comes home to claim the girl in the final sequence. The light and joyful tone of Henry's wooing, distasteful though some find it today, would doubtless have been felt to be in keeping with the 'happy ending' of the traditional comic genre by those who first witnessed it. The overtones of sexual bawdry would also have contributed, as we have seen, to the atmosphere of prospective procreation with which the action closes; how much significance should be attached to the fact that the union between Henry and Katharine produced the ill-fated Henry VI will depend on the stance we adopt towards other elements already discussed. Coming events do not necessarily have to cast their shadow over the finale of *Henry V*.

One article of recent years which adopts a reasonably optimistic view of the play is William Babula's 'Whatever Happened to Prince Hal?' This critic locates the play's theme in the common Renaissance topos of the maturation of a ruler, a concept which can be found occupying the attention of countless Elizabethan playwrights, at a period when the sovereign's political and emotional wisdom had profound implications for the fortunes of the realm. Babula sees *Henry V* as embodying a fresh start for the character known from the two parts of *Henry IV* as Prince Hal, so that by this reading Henry is portrayed in the opening acts as a young man in desperate need of learning to temper his passionate quest for glory and honour and his ardent rhetoric with a measure of moderation. Henry's tendency to persuade somebody else to 'carry the can' for his decisions is no longer viewed as potentially tragic in its implications; rather it is something that experience will eventually teach the king to abandon as he grows to maturity. For this reason, considerable importance is again attached to the fifth act and the wooing of Kate:

The change in Henry is particularly signified by the change in his language. He once spoke in epic rhetoric concerning war, he now speaks in simple prose as he pleads his love. In fact he insists upon an honesty of style; he is not covering anything with art. This is certainly different from the Henry we saw before . . . There is no longer a distance between words and reality, a distance we felt so keenly between the words of the Chorus and the realities of the action . . . At the end of the play both king and Chorus eschew the rhetorical language with which they disguised facts. Art has been stripped off and the reality remains. At the close of the play Henry is honest and peaceseeking; he has matured as monarch and man.

Henry V

In this way the critic, while not refusing to recognize the defects and anomalies in Henry's conduct and attitudes, is able to reconcile them with Shakespeare's evident perception of positive qualities in his hero, and so present us with a theme which unifies the text in the way that many other readings do not.

But perhaps the most interesting effort made in recent years to attempt to rationalize the argument between those who see the play as a positive affirmation of what Henry stands for and those who emphasize the negative nature of his achievements is found in Norman Rabkin's article, 'Rabbits, Ducks, and *Henry V*', in *Shakespeare Quarterly* (Summer 1977). Rabkin's title alludes to the famous optical image used in psychological experiments which can be interpreted as either a rabbit or a duck depending on which 'meaning' of the drawing is allowed to predominate. Rabkin argues that *Henry V* works in this manner: one can, if one chooses, highlight the positive elements in the play, those which build up the image of the king as an ideal monarch in whose epic achievements we are invited to take pride, or one can regard Henry as a remorseless and two-faced war-monger whose presentation is tinged with irony, satire and even disgust. Rabkin's article seeks to establish a positive principle of artistic creativity out of the play's undoubted ambiguities and ambivalences by giving full value to both sets of elements, arguing that in this play, 'Shakespeare creates a work whose ultimate power is precisely the fact that it points in two opposite directions, virtually daring us to choose one of the two opposed interpretations it requires of us.' Sensing that the only adequate summation of what had preceded *Henry V* in the dramatic trilogy which it concludes had to be cast in ambivalent form, Rabkin sees the positive interpretation of the play as more in tune with the spirit of *1 Henry IV*, while the values of *2 Henry IV* are more adequately reflected if we adopt the negative position, and goes on to demonstrate that:

Henry V is brilliantly capable of being read, fully and subtly, as each of the plays the two parts of *Henry IV* had respectively anticipated. Leaving the theatre at the end of the first performance, some members of the audience knew that they had seen a rabbit, others a duck. Still others, and I would suggest that they were Shakespeare's best audience, knew terrifyingly that they did not know what to think.

Rabkin writes appreciatively of the play's excitements of language and personality, and does ample justice to Henry's inspirational leadership as well as his gift for understanding both himself and others, so that he becomes 'the epitome of what the cycle has taught us to value as best in a monarch, indeed in a man', 'a personality integrated in itself

Masterstudies: Henry V

and ready to bring unity and joy to a realm that has suffered long from rule by men less at ease with themselves and less able to identify their own interests with those of their country.' Yet the critic articulates equally clearly the other side of the coin: the way in which the comedy of the close is clouded by our prior knowledge of what the tragic sequel will be, the doubts which bedevil the justice of the royal claim to France, Henry's own character weaknesses and acts of questionable probity, 'the reality of the post-war world the play so powerfully conjures up'. However, the article concludes that to hold either of these views exclusively does an injustice to the play's rich complexity, yet that to hold them simultaneously – that is to say, as a study of contradictory impulses in one man – is unconvincingly uncommitted. Rabkin sees Shakespeare himself as personally torn between the two Henries, perhaps between the one he hoped was so, and the one he feared was so, and argues that such a stance conforms to the inner feelings of all of us when confronted by the world of political values, torn 'between our longing that authority figures can be like us and our suspicion that they must have traded away their inwardness for the sake of power':

The play contrasts our hope that society can solve our problems with our knowledge that society has never done so. The inscrutability of *Henry V* is the inscrutability of history.

In this wide sea of speculations and interpretations the novice reader is perhaps more likely to sink than to float, but the debate at least demonstrates the rich variety of themes which may be discovered in what is sometimes reckoned to be one of Shakespeare's least complex and least baffling plays. We can if we choose regard the work as one in which a human being in a position of authority abuses his position, or one where he redeems himself from his former errors through laying aside his authority in order to identify with the perils and pangs of his subordinates. Some see Henry as humanized by his contact with his common soldiers, others sense that he is only playing the part of a populist monarch before Agincourt and after, just as they feel his performance as a simple-hearted plain-spoken wooer in the final scene to be bogus. Many others acknowledge Henry's greatness of spirit and lightness of heart, but consider these achieved at the cost not only of his better instincts, but at the expense of his former cronies in enjoyment of life's more convivial pleasures. However their felonious and cowardly antics may undercut the glorious heroics of Henry's campaign, Bardolph, Nym and Pistol in their anarchic parody of military honour cast a very human light on the pursuit of glory, and their function is surely to supply one more approach to the central topic of war. In including these figures in

Henry V

Henry V, even without Falstaff as their former presiding genius, the playwright is able to suggest that while individual bravery and self-sacrifice are not to be despised, yet they are not to be regarded as the be-all and end-all of human achievement. There is a rich humanity in the chastened figure of Pistol, and a defiance in his exit lines in Act V, Scene 1 which reminds us that even hero-kings do not inspire all their followers to deeds of high renown. Even the scum of the earth has his role in the kingdom Henry has informed with a new sense of purpose. Our unwilling admiration for Pistol's ability to survive may have a bearing on our attitude to Henry himself, and on the way we respond to Shakespeare's most thorough-going exploration of the ambivalence of warfare and of the human qualities which it brings to the fore.

The Play in the Theatre

Despite an assumed dearth of prestigious parts and its apparent demand for spectacular staging, *Henry V* has proved a consistently popular play in the English repertoire, even at periods when one might assume that its heroic rhetoric and martial sentiments would be alien to the prevailing sensibilities of the age. At times of national stress – during the Napoleonic campaigns, or the traumatic British defeats marking the start of the Boer War, or the weeks leading up to the 'Munich Crisis' – true appreciation of its qualities has been hampered by its being treated as a work of patriotic piety, but it is less easy to account for its appeal throughout, say, the post-war years, which have seen at least half a dozen notably successful productions in Britain alone. Since Olivier's film appearance, the roll-call of memorable Henries has included Paul Scofield, the late Richard Burton, Christopher Plummer, Donald Houston, Ian Holm, Alan Howard, Michael Williams and Kenneth Branagh, yet in almost every case it has been the play as a whole which appears to have exerted the greater persuasive pressure on the public, rather than the star in isolation, as was the case up until World War I. If the ultimate test of a play's quality is whether or not potential spectators are still prepared to pay to watch it, then *Henry V* obviously passes that test with banners flying.

No contemporary records of performances of the drama have survived, though the First Quarto's title page assures us that the text is printed 'As it hath bene sundry times playd', which has offered the textual scholars some food for thought, as we have seen. A hint as to the piece's early popularity is possibly conveyed by the existence of three separate quarto editions prior to the play's appearance in the First Folio of 1623, though it is fair to note that *Richard II* and *Richard III* ran to five and six quartos respectively. We learn little of the play's fate during the first half of the seventeenth century, up to the closure of the play-houses in 1642, but that Henry and his deeds remained of theatrical interest following the Restoration of 1660 is clear. It is significant that the first dramatic work by Roger Boyle, first Earl of Orrery (1621–79), to be staged was his *History of Henry the Fifth*, witnessed on 13 August 1664 by Samuel Pepys, who confided to his diary that the drama was 'the most full of height and raptures of wit and sense, that ever I heard'. If Shakespeare's piece had not actually created an audience for Boyle's, the nobleman certainly seems to have taken pains to avoid the charge so often levelled against the playwrights contemporary with him who sought to beautify themselves with Shakespeare's feathers: only one scene in Boyle's play, where the lords of England and France discuss the niceties of Salic law in rhymed couplets, suggests Shakespearean inspiration, while the plot itself centres on the rivalry in love of Owen Tudor and King Henry for the hand of the French princess. If we give the earl credit for avoiding mere Shakespearean imitation, we must admit that the result is rather tame and frigid.

The same must be said of Aaron Hill's far less independent rendering of *Henry V*, set forth in 1723 without any of the original comic creations, it is true, but with plentiful use made of the sentiments and diction of Shakespeare's piece. While the interest of the play is again shifted almost completely towards the romantic plane, Hill retains the figures of Cambridge, Scroop and Grey, whose plotting forms a central feature of the action, and which is linked to the sexual interest through Harriet, an invented character who is both Scroop's niece and a former mistress of the king. The princess saves Henry from the conspirators; Harriet's resentment at the king's treatment of her is melted and she commits suicide: the way is cleared for a happy dénouement. The action at Agincourt is retained, but most of the rest of the piece takes place before Harfleur, in keeping with the neo-classical predisposition for dramatic action to be confined to as unified a setting as possible. The essence of plays of the period lay in concentration and symmetry, but one does not have to adulate *Henry V* (as does George Odell) as a 'manly, heroic play' to deplore the sentimental travesty that Aaron Hill makes of it.

In the succeeding century, productions of the play were not uncommon, although *Henry V* appears never to have rivalled the popularity of its predecessor *1 Henry IV*, where Falstaff's perennial appeal made any production a sure-fire success. On 6 July 1668 Pepys recorded Betterton's return to the stage as Henry V after an illness, but there is no further performance of the piece noted in the records until it was revived at Covent Garden on 23 February 1738, when it was billed as 'Not Acted these Forty Years'. The part of Henry was played on this occasion by an Irish actor, Dennis Delane, whose previous roles had included Othello, Hotspur, Richard III, Brutus, Macbeth and Lear. At Covent Garden he added Falstaff, King John and Richard II to his repertoire, and at Drury Lane he appeared as Shylock and Hamlet. He sounds as though he was a cultured and good-looking actor, better suited to wellbred than heroic parts, which must have made his Henry a somewhat unequal performance, but he continued to play the king at intervals for the rest of his career, until his untimely death in 1750.

Masterstudies: Henry V

His successor as the best Henry of the age was another Irish actor, Spranger Barry who, like Delane, served his theatrical apprenticeship in Dublin before making his mark in London. At the time of his first appearance in the role (at Drury Lane on 16 December 1747), the international rivalry between England and France had intensified to such an extent that the topicality of Shakespeare's drama was being exploited by theatrical managers everywhere. On 19 April 1744 a Covent Garden presentation 'reviv'd by particular desire' – France had declared war the previous month – was embellished with two musical items, the songs 'To Arms' and 'Britons, strike home'. At Drury Lane on 4 August 1746 an afterpiece entitled *The Conspiracy Discover'd; or, French Policy Defeated* was staged, described as 'An Historical Dramatic Piece of one act (taken from Shakespear) with a representation of the Trials of the Lords for High Treason, in the Reign of King Henry V'. The adaptation was made to exploit the topical interest in the trial of three peers of the realm for their participation in the Jacobite Rebellion of 1745. Up until the 1790s long runs of *Henry V* occurred, often embellished in the playbills with such phrases as, 'With the glorious Victory of the English against the French at the Battle of Agincourt', and when Richard Wroughton starred as Henry for the first time at Covent Garden on 11 May 1778, the piece was boldly subtitled *The Conquest of France*, a device adopted eleven years later by John Philip Kemble when he made his debut in the part at Drury Lane. Shakespeare's piece was still being conscripted in the cause of national unity.

Spranger Barry, like Dennis Delane, was recognized as a 'manly actor' when he opened in *Henry V* in 1747: he had a fine figure and possessed a voice 'the harmony and melody of whose silver tones were resistless' according to contemporary opinion. In Dublin he had played a range of parts including Hotspur, Lear and Henry, and it was under the auspices of David Garrick, the leading English actor of the day, that Barry came to appear at Drury Lane under Garrick's management, the pair alternating roles in a number of classic plays, including *Hamlet* and *Macbeth*. However, an almost inevitable rivalry developed between the two men, but not before Barry had made a hit as Henry V at Garrick's theatre, the manager contenting himself with appearing as the Chorus. Charles Macklin, the finest Shylock of his day, made a noteworthy Fluellen.

Barry quitted Garrick's company at the end of the 1749–50 season, and betook himself, Mrs Cibber and Charles Macklin (who had played Juliet and Mercutio, respectively, to his Romeo) to the rival establishment at Covent Garden. Here he continued to take the lead in productions of *Henry V*, which saw the boards of the Covent Garden stage in every season but two between 1754 and 1770, Barry last playing the role in 1758, the year he migrated back to Dublin to enter management on his own account. Barry's handsome face and athletic figure, together with his 'silver' voice which made his Romeo so much superior to that of Garrick when Drury Lane and Covent Garden mounted competing productions of the tragedy in 1750, no doubt made him a striking Henry; it was clearly not a part that the more intelligent and animated Garrick ever aspired to.

Barry enjoyed a nine-year reign as Henry, but the dominating actor in the part during the latter half of the eighteenth century was William Smith, usually referred to as 'Gentleman Smith', on account of his Eton and Cambridge background, his fondness for riding and hunting, and his marriage to a peer's daughter. A protégé of Spranger Barry, his first appearance as Henry came at the age of about twenty-five, on 18 February 1755 at Covent Garden, where he also enjoyed success as Orlando, Romeo, Hotspur, Edgar in *King Lear*, Hamlet, Coriolanus, Richard III and Macbeth. In 1774 he transferred his affections to Drury Lane, where he added the character of the Duke in *Measure for Measure* to his Shakespearean range, and created the part of Charles Surface in Sheridan's *The School for Scandal* on 8 May 1777. When the celebrated Sarah Siddons made her London debut as Lady Macbeth – her most memorable role – on 2 February 1785, Smith played opposite her. With his polished manners, 'pleasing person', powerful voice and grace of movement, Smith was perhaps the ideal Henry, excelling too as Hamlet, Hotspur and Edgar, in all of whose personalities a strong element of the heroic is important. Even the qualities which went to make him a notable performer in comedies of manners such as *The Beaux' Stratagem* and *The School for Scandal* must have helped to temper the more ruthless and severe traits in Henry V when 'Gentleman Smith' portrayed him.

The productions in which Barry and Smith found fame not only took advantage of the patriotic sentiments they aroused, but also of the opportunities for scenic display they invited. Though never approaching the grandiose spectacles of the following century, eighteenth-century Shakespeare was rarely barren of decorative devices, and *Henry V* in particular was frequently accompanied by such incitements to national pride as the representation of an English coronation which embellished performances at both playhouses for almost a decade. Pageantry of various kinds was a constant feature of classical dramatic productions and one may sense that magnificent costumes and splendid banners often had to compensate for plain and sparsely furnished settings until the craze for lavish display set in towards the end of the eighteenth century, and so led to the heavily upholstered presentations made fashionable by the great Victorian actor–managers.

Masterstudies: Henry V

Henry V appears to have suffered less frequently than many Shakespearean plays in the seventeenth and eighteenth centuries from the extensive cutting of its characters and scenes, though a number of acting editions of the period omit all the Chorus's speeches. However, many of the cast lists which feature on contemporary playbills name this character and the actor designated to play the role, which suggests that some at least of the Chorus's lines were retained. Garrick certainly appeared in the part in 1747 and 1748, and at Covent Garden the Chorus was often presented by Lacy Ryan, a veteran of the stage, affected with 'a drawling, croaking accent', the result of being shot in the jaw by a robber. Thus, assertions that the Chorus was not restored until Macready's production of June 1839 must be treated warily.

By the time 'Gentleman Smith' retired in 1788, another Henry had taken his place at Covent Garden in the shape of Richard Wroughton, who first played the part on 11 May 1778, when, we are told, the 'Original *Chorus*' was spoken by one Hull. Wroughton, just thirty when he first essayed Henry, had made his reputation in youthful roles such as Claudio in *Measure for Measure*, Florizel, Sebastian, Romeo and Don Pedro in *Much Ado About Nothing*, though like most leading actors of his day he also appeared in more mature parts such as Lear and Othello. Wroughton does not sound to have been the ideal Henry: we learn that his voice was unprepossessing, his face round and inexpressive, and that he was knock-kneed. However, Michael Kelly, the Irish actor and singer, spoke of him as being 'a sterling, sound, and sensible performer', and presumably these qualities all went to the making of his Henry V. However, on 1 October 1789 he was superseded in the public estimation by one of the noblest and most imposing actors of his generation, when John Philip Kemble undertook the role at Drury Lane, appearing in an adaptation of the text made by himself.

Kemble was the brother of Sarah Siddons and, by comparison with the average actor of his time, a well-educated man. Born into a theatrical family, Kemble gained his early experience in York and then appeared at Drury Lane in such key parts as Hamlet, Richard III, King John, Othello and Lear. One of his achievements was said to have been to persuade Sheridan, then manager at the theatre, to costume the company's repertoire in clothing more true to the periods in which the plays were set. This concern for antiquarian accuracy was to become overdone in the following century, but at the start it marked a great advance in theatrical sophistication. In 1788 Kemble succeeded Sheridan as manager at Drury Lane, and one of his earliest triumphs at his own playhouse was as Henry V. James Boaden in his *Life*, published in 1825, claimed that:

The Play in the Theatre

As a *coup de Theatre*, his starting up from prayer at the sound of the trumpet, in the passage where he states his attempted atonement to Richard the Second, formed one of the most spirited excitements that the stage has ever displayed. His occasional reversions to the 'mad wag', the 'sweet young prince', had a singular charm, as the condescension of one who could be so terrible.

Similarly, the *Prompter* for 4 November 1789 found something awe-inspiring and sombre in the actor's rendition of the role: 'Kemble's invocation to the Deity has such a solemnity and earnestness, added to a hearty devotion, that exalts the soul and fills it with reverence.'

We might now be inclined to feel that *Henry V* suffered more than it gained from Kemble's revivifying touch; his style of delivery was said to have been heavily declamatory and stately, and he certainly loved to load his productions with pageants and processions wherever he could. Moreover, he was prepared to take liberties with Shakespeare's texts in order to make them conform to the artistic standards of regularity and classical formality which the late eighteenth century demanded. Yet undoubtedly his Henry was a success: he appeared in the role on ten occasions in the 1789-90 season, and acted the part for five consecutive seasons thereafter. In 1801 he could be found in the part at Drury Lane, in 1811 at Covent Garden.

Whether Kemble's later presentations of the piece reflected a desire for greater historical accuracy is unclear, but a reviewer in the *Monthly Mirror* for December 1801 was sceptical of the degree of success then achieved in the sets and costumes: Kemble appears to have worn a jerkin, cloak, boots and gloves of the reign of Charles I, but an Elizabethan cap with 'an odd sort of crown stuck round its brims', together with the riband of the George, dating from Henry VIII's time! Pistol wore a modern cocked hat, and the bishops, contemporary gowns with lawn sleeves. The Boar's Head took the form of a modern inn, while the painted view of Southampton incorporated modern ships and a lighthouse.

Possibly Kemble or his scene-painter wished to emphasize what was felt to be the play's contemporary relevance for a nation locked in combat with its traditional continental rival. In 1803, Covent Garden staged the piece in aid of the Patriotic Fund, while a performance in Manchester the following year led the *Townsman*'s dramatic critic to draw attention to the play's 'loyal sentiments' and the description of 'one of our greatest victories over the French', the Henry being so moved by the occasion as to exhort his troops, at the end of the speech before Harfleur, to 'Cry God for Harry, England, and *King George*!'

Edmund Kean, the greatest actor of the ensuing period, only attempted to play Henry V once, breaking down on the Drury Lane stage on

Masterstudies: Henry V

8 March 1830, and being unable to complete the performance. It was left to the more sober but less charismatic William Charles Macready to supply the age with its finest Henry in a series of portrayals culminating in a splendidly elaborate revival at Covent Garden on 10 June 1839, which is fortunately well-documented.

The haughty and imperious Macready helped purge the Regency stage of some of its worst excesses, while bequeathing to his successors some excesses of his own. In the field of Shakespeare he did much to reintroduce to the theatre the substance of the original texts, which had been cut by previous managements: for example, his *King Lear* staged in January 1838 restored the part of the Fool, albeit played by a woman, and cut the interpolated love affair between Edgar and Cordelia, *de rigueur* until then. If Macready did not precisely resurrect the Chorus speeches in *Henry V*, he certainly made them prominent, having them spoken by George Vandenhoff in the person of Time, 'russet-bearded, with scythe and glass': an allegorical tableau at the start of the piece showed Henry with the figures of Famine, Fire and War at his heels.

This tendency to illustrate the text literally wherever possible was found most markedly developed in the choric scenes; to quote Macready's programme note:

To impress more strongly on the auditor, and render still more palpable those portions of the story which have not the advantage of action, and still are requisite to the drama's completeness, the narrative and descriptive poetry spoken by the Chorus is accompanied with Pictorial Illustrations from the pen of Mr Stanfield.

The Times for 11 June 1839 gives a vivid impression of Macready's innovations:

As a scenic spectacle the play of *Henry V*, as produced last night, merits unqualified praise, and we scarcely know whether most to admire the care, taste, and research displayed in the design, or the beauty of the execution . . . the third act was ushered in by a moving diorama, by far the most splendid piece of scenery presented on the occasion. The English fleet is seen leaving Southampton, its course is traced across the sea, and the audience are gradually brought to the siege of Harfleur. By an ingenious arrangement the business of the act begins before the diorama has quite passed, and the picture, as it were, melts away into the actual siege by the characters. The grouping, confusion and truth of this scene is excellently managed. Another moving diorama, representing the French and English camps prior to the battle of Agincourt, introduced the fourth act, and another of the King's triumphal entry into London, brought in the fifth. Here, and indeed the whole of the scenery, was beautifully painted; but the siege of Harfleur was the grand point. The battle of Agincourt produced no effect . . .

The Play in the Theatre

Some objections to 'over-embellishment' were voiced, but generally Macready's way with the play continued in vogue well into the present century; if productions in the 1700s had stressed the patriotic parallels, from Macready onwards *Henry V* was primarily valued for what an actor–manager could make of the opportunities for surrounding himself with scenes of spectacular grandeur.

Antiquarian accuracy was the watchword of Charles Kean, nicknamed by *Punch* 'the Great Upholsterer', whose massive productions at the Princess's Theatre were noted for the thoroughness of the historical research that went into them and for the number of 'supers' or extras employed in their crowd scenes, on some occasions as many as five or six hundred. Kean's *Henry V*, staged on 28 March 1859, followed the Macready trail, though with even more concern for archaeological exactitude: Kean, the Eton-educated son of the great Edmund, sought to instruct as well as entertain, and drew on contemporary accounts for the fine details of his crowd and battle scenes, supporting his claim that he had never 'permitted historical truth to be sacrificed to mere theatrical effect'. The siege of Harfleur included copies of fifteenth-century artillery; Henry's entry into London – the highlight of Kean's presentation – featured a hymn 'supposed to be as old as AD 1310'. A contemporary print shows the victorious monarch on a richly caparisoned horse riding beneath a tower from which a shower of gold is scattered by a group of angels on the ramparts, while a bevy of virgins mob the king below. Henry's route is lined with bearded prophets, singing boys, kings, martyrs and confessors, while on either side the citizens of London cheer and wave their hats in great profusion. Notable is the animated group thronging the rigging of a ship anchored in the Thames. Small wonder that Charles Kean's wife, Ellen Tree, spoke the choruses in the character of Clio, the Muse of History!

Other Victorian productions – notably that of Samuel Phelps, who played the King at Sadler's Wells in 1852 – were less overwhelming affairs, but 'pictorial Shakespeare' persisted for at least another sixty years, as did vast crowd scenes, even modest Phelps attaching to each of his forty soldiers marching across the stage two waxwork dummies from Madame Tussaud's in order to swell their ranks. He probably imported fewer 'supers' to Windsor Castle for his command performance there on 10 November 1853, though the royal pleasure had he done so might have been heightened, for Queen Victoria found his way of impersonating the King 'rather heavy'. She had already viewed Macready's production in 1839, commenting favourably on the scenery but irritated by Katharine's broken English and the excessive appearances of Fluellen.

Masterstudies: Henry V

Twenty years later she and Albert visited Kean's mammoth production four times in three months.

A further twenty years had passed when Augustus Harris inaugurated his managerial reign at Drury Lane with *Henry V*; the basis for this presentation was that of Charles Calvert who staged the play in Manchester in September 1872, continuing the Macready–Kean tradition of interpolated, 'historically authentic' tableaux of the field of Agincourt and Henry's triumphant return to London, the latter involving some three hundred extras. The production transferred to New York where Henry James saw it, deploring the attempt to achieve absolute scenic verisimilitude, but approving of George Rignold's performance as the king; eventually the piece was given at Drury Lane on 1 November 1879, with a cast that found room for a number of horses, including the monarch's white charger, Crispin. Of the dashing, virile Rignold, Dutton Cook wrote in *Nights at the Play* (1883):

He is most heroically pugnacious of aspect; he looks a born leader of fighting men; he exhibits indefatigable vigour alike as swordsman and orator; he overwhelms his foes both by force of arms and strength of lungs. As, falchion in hand, clothed in complete steel, with a richly emblazoned tabard, he stands in that spot so prized by the histrionic mind, the exact centre of the stage ... he presents as striking a stage figure as I think I ever saw ... Of course subtlety of interpretation was not required; Henry V is not an intellectual character.

Rignold's worldwide success (he later emigrated to Australia) and Cook's closing sneer suggest that the role of Henry was by this time felt to be the exclusive preserve of good-looking actors whose presence and vigour suggested the heroic stereotype rather than a man possessed of any individuality: it is notable that neither Henry Irving nor Herbert Beerbohm Tree, the outstanding theatrical personalities of the late Victorian and Edwardian era, ever attempted to play the part. Of those who did, F. R. Benson and Lewis Waller stand out. Benson, whose company was the mainstay of the Stratford-on-Avon Shakespeare Festival from 1886 until 1919, first played Henry on 22 April 1897 in a production which omitted the Chorus in favour of the limited amount of spectacle (including singing, and dancing-girls in the French camp) Benson's budget would allow, and continued in the title role until well into his sixties.

When he took over the Lyceum for a season from Irving on 15 February 1900, Benson embarked with this play, possibly to raise the capital's spirits after the military reverses Britain had suffered at the hands of the Boers; London presumably thrilled to the athletic player's celebrated spear-vault in full armour on to the ramparts of Harfleur, though surprisingly *The Times* found the actor 'hardly robust enough ... There is too much sense of effort in his performance ...' and Max Beerbohm was wittily critical of the cast's qualifications, though one senses that he did not care for the choice of play in the first place: 'It should be done brilliantly, splendidly, or not at all. Only the best kind of acting, and the best kind of production, could make it anything but tedious.' Yet W. B. Yeats, who saw Benson as Henry at Stratford only a year later, admired the way he 'kept that somewhat crude King ... from becoming vulgar in the love scene at the end', 'which Mr Waller *did not*'. Some years later W. Bridges-Adams wrote of Benson, 'nobility was the making of his Henry V. Waller's (unsurpassed) was the more *ringing* performance; but in the prayer F.R.B. really made you feel that he was in communion with God.'

Lewis Waller, who was just forty when he first played Henry on 22 December 1900, was like George Rignold the physical embodiment of manly grace, energy and panache, and he too revived the role on many subsequent occasions. Among his earlier Shakespearean successes were Hotspur, Laertes and Brutus for Beerbohm Tree, and he created the part of Sir Robert Chiltern in Wilde's *An Ideal Husband*. Henry was reckoned to be his finest part; even Beerbohm enjoyed a performance of which a modern theatre historian, J. C. Trewin, has written:

Waller saw Henry as a star of England almost a shooting star. When he hurtled downstage in the swell of the Crispin speech, swinging round to speak the final lines with his back to the house and his men facing him in a semicircle, the audience rose at him. Waller needed strong, plain effects. He lacked Benson's jetting imagination, but he could sound a fanfare, and he gave to the staging of *Henry V* a suitable glow and flourish without turning it to an over-populated battle-piece from a Victorian canvas ... It was probably the most theatrical *Henry V* in record.

By the time Waller died in November 1915 the days of elaborate Victorian-style Shakespeare were over, and with the successive departures of the greatest of the Edwardian actor–managers, public interest shifted towards the production as an artistic totality and away from the personal charisma of the leading player, even though stars remained in demand. The post-war trend in stage design was towards a greater degree of simplification and stylization in the presentation of the English classics, and it was noteworthy that when W. Bridges-Adams produced the play at Stratford on 28 July 1920 and brought it to London the following October, the majority of the episodes were set forth 'in panel form between sliding curtains', winning the acclaim of the doyen of theatrical revolutionaries, William Poel, who had long pioneered the use of simple

Masterstudies: Henry V

curtained settings, unencumbered with heavily realistic and unwieldy scenery which rendered Shakespeare's word-pictures redundant. Poel had himself presented *Henry V* at a special Stratford matinée on 23 October 1901; now his methods were becoming far more acceptable to audiences inclined to view Edwardian elaboration with distaste. In 1920 Robert Atkins, a disciple of Poel, took over at the Old Vic, and made use of a semi-permanent Elizabethan-style stage with a small platform jutting out from it; 'scenery' as such was cut down to a bare minimum in order that swiftness and simplicity should become the keynotes of the 'house style'. In such a manner and on such a stage Atkins presented *Henry V* in the 1921–2 season, maintaining the tradition of a female Chorus as had Waller, but presenting Shakespeare's text virtually intact. His successor at the Old Vic, Andrew Leigh (Atkins's Fluellen), directed the play as part of the 1928–9 programme, with Sybil Thorndike as an Elizabethan-boy Chorus and her husband Lewis Casson in the lead. In 1934 came two productions, one by Stanley Bell at the Alhambra, with Godfrey Tearle as Henry, the other at Stratford with John Wyse and Robert Atkins again in charge. Two years later Atkins achieved his ambition to direct on an open stage when he leased a boxing stadium at Blackfriars, and with Hubert Gregg as his king, staged the play 'under a hard white light, with the audience on three sides' on a platform backed by an inner stage and a balcony. In September 1938, Ivor Novello, the popular composer of and leading performer in lavish Drury Lane musicals, made an unexpectedly successful Shakespearean debut in the part of Henry, in a spectacular but effective production by Lewis Casson. Again a woman (Gwen Ffrangcon-Davies) played the Chorus, dressed as a nimble pageboy, and there was something like a return to Macready's manner with soldiers entering Harfleur (to a Novello march!), a ship-filled Southampton scene and an impressive array of arms and banners at Agincourt itself. With a European war threatened, *Henry V* had once again acted as something of a national rallying-point, though the 'Crisis' terminated the run prematurely.

But undoubtedly the best presentation between the wars was Tyrone Guthrie's Old Vic version of April 1937, produced with the imminent coronation of King George VI in mind. Neither Guthrie nor Olivier, his Henry, cared much for the play; nevertheless the right patriotic note was evidently struck, Olivier found the key to the character in the poetry, and Motley's décor, with its use of massed banners in silver, red and blue, was highly praised. The supporting cast numbered over a hundred, reinforced by a dozen sopranos from Sadler's Wells Opera for the full choral finale. Marius Goring, and later Michael Redgrave, played the Chorus, reclaiming the role from the women; the cast included Harcourt

The Play in the Theatre

Williams as the King of France, a part he recreated for Olivier's film version some years later – and it is significant that the smaller roles were beginning to be noticed. Of Olivier's king, Audrey Williamson wrote in *Old Vic Drama* (1948):

Few soldiers would not have plunged into the breach after this Henry. The note of majesty was struck at the start ... One sensed the greyhound straining at the leash, and when the cannon burst it loosed thunder and lightning. The scenes with Williams and Kate on the other hand were played with a delightful humour, and none of the lighter touches of humanity or wit was missed.

For many Olivier's (and Guthrie's) Henry has remained the definitive rendition.

Of the many portrayals and productions of the years since Olivier directed his film adaptation, there is only space to mention a handful of outstanding examples. Dorothy Green's 1946 Stratford presentation with Paul Scofield was felt by many to be too muted and Scofield's performance too tentative for total success. In 1951 the play was staged (as so often) to boost a national occasion, in this instance the Festival of Britain, and in two productions actors more suited by temperament to the part of Shakespeare's king than Scofield offered the public their interpretations. Alec Clunes directed by Glen Byam Shaw at the Old Vic suggested a thoughtful, conscientious – sometimes conscience-stricken – leader, more in tune with the somewhat chastened spirit of post-war Britain than Olivier's vibrant squadron leader. At Stratford-on-Avon, appearing in a tetralogy in which he first emerged as Prince Hal, Richard Burton was dismissed by many as too cold and detached, although Robert Speaight felt that with 'a secret purpose plain to read in his steady gaze' he took 'much of the callousness out of Hal and much of the chauvinism out of Harry'. Burton's narrow vocal range was adversely criticized, being compared unfavourably with Redgrave's energetic delivery as the Chorus, but Ivor Brown warmed to the actor's lack of rhetorical bravura: 'This is a human believable King, if not a soloist "obliging" on the clarion.' Burton was to confess in later years that he found himself 'incapable of playing such a role', but on 13 December 1955 under Michael Benthall's direction at the Old Vic he scored a far greater triumph, *The Times* writing of his 'steely strength which becomes the martial ring and hard brilliance of the patriotic verse'. Kenneth Tynan spoke in the *Observer* of 'a cunning warrior, stocky and astute, unafraid of harshness or of curling the royal lip'.

Clunes and Burton certainly helped to initiate a trend in persuading actors and directors away from 'the Happy Warrior' conception of Henry's character, towards that more ambivalent and even self-doubting

Masterstudies: Henry V

figure, veering between ruthlessness and vulnerability, which has dominated both the stage and literary criticism since the mid-fifties. Such a portrait may seem to be consistent with the increasing British distrust of heroics since the Suez Crisis of 1956, but perhaps Burton overdid the Machiavellian traits in Henry's make-up, although this too would accord well with modern historical assessments. However, the king must be endowed with some marks of personal appeal or the play is thrown out of balance, and this has remained one of the central problems in productions of the last thirty years. In 1964, when the Royal Shakespeare Company presented the entire sequence of histories from *Richard II* to *Richard III*, Ian Holm played a king young in years and short in stature, whose dogged heroism bore signs of the desperate tenacity of fatigue, who identified himself only too completely with the fortunes of his troops. In a series of productions by Peter Hall and John Barton intended to expose the nature of *realpolitik*, Robert Speaight saw Holm as 'an essentially democratic Henry, almost as tattered and mud-bespattered as the "Old Contemptibles" with whom he marched; discovering his kingship within himself and through his comradeship with other men'. At other points in the action this interpretation undermined the king's authority, but it gave greater point to an allusion which sometimes lacks sincerity – 'We few, we happy few, we band of brothers' gained fresh poignancy: this Henry worked personally for his victories in France. On the other hand, one could rarely feel that this king would *inspire* his followers to victory. This sovereign was thoughtful, sober and at times grim; as John Russell Brown wrote in *Shakespeare Survey*, 'he never attempted to enter the outline depicted by the Chorus of "cheerful semblance and sweet majesty..." or "A largess universal, like the sun." Amid the gunsmoke and the blood-stained corpses Holm's Henry waded dourly on.'

Equally interesting, but in a different vein, was Alan Howard who played the part in a centenary production at Stratford, directed by Terry Hands, first seen on 31 March 1975, a presentation well documented by Sally Beauman, complete with textual alterations (1976). Taking his cue from the opening Chorus speech, Hands raised some eyebrows by beginning the action with his cast assembling on stage dressed in rehearsal-gear – tracksuits and jeans – and creating the play through stimulating the audience's imaginations, the 'costume element' only being built up gradually as the play unfolded. Such a determinedly 'anti-illusionistic' opening was quickly supplanted in the mind by some striking scenic effects, notably the device of suspending canopies decorated with heraldic escutcheons over the scenes of preparation and diplomacy, which were lowered for the battles to produce grey and brown landscapes of war,

The Play in the Theatre

timeless in their application, but too many spectators still demanded to know what 'the footballers' of the opening were 'supposed to represent'.

Of Howard's hero, similar but more informed reservations were expressed; Richard David summed matters up well when he wrote in *Shakespeare in the Theatre* (1978):

> The peculiarity of *Henry V* is that it is concerned with a concept, the quality of kingship or more precisely of heroic leadership, that in a generation disillusioned by two world wars is thought by some to have become suspect. At any rate the theory among certain directors, as well as critics, seems to be that Harry the fifth is only a hero if he is a reluctant hero.

For David, therefore, Howard's Henry 'was certainly not what I imagine Shakespeare intended him to be, a natural, born leader', a point Harold Hobson's *Sunday Times* review reinforced:

> ... he used once to be played as a great king and noble warrior comforting his people: but today we see him, Alan Howard plays him, as a man sorely in need of comfort himself, and knowing that he will have to do his best in a terrible situation without it ... Mr Howard's superb, and I had almost said eclipsing, Henry is not a natural soldier. Whenever war approaches, doubts and distress cloud Mr Howard's face: his Henry is made for other things than war. He fears war: but being in it he acquits himself like a pride of lions ...

Scrupulous, uncertain, haunted by his responsibilities in letting the dogs of war slip, this Henry (like Ian Holm's before him) seemed less 'one of them' and more 'one of us'.

More recently has come Adrian Noble's production at Stratford which opened on 22 March 1984, where, as in Terry Hands's presentation, the contrast between the French resplendently attired in opulent golds and blacks and the English in more pragmatic browns and duns, sheltering under tarpaulins from the torrential autumn rains, was visually impressive. Kenneth Branagh's performance as the king seemed conceived on similar lines to Howard's, except that it was now Henry's youth and inexperience in combat that were stressed. 'Brisk, sprightly, and sensitive', in the words of Nicholas Shrimpton in *Shakespeare Survey* 38, Branagh like Holm presented a lad forced to mature rapidly in the hard school of combat, so that the two seemingly contradictory aspects of the historical reality that was Henry seemed to be concurrently present. To quote Shrimpton again, 'The sensitive boy-king who shrank from atrocities was seen to be, simultaneously, the noble leader of an inspired crusade and the commander of a ruthless gang of raggle-taggle mercenaries.' But a Henry who fainted from excitement before Harfleur and burst into tears at Bardolph's execution was worlds away from the glad confident mornings of Charles Kean or Lewis Waller.

Conclusion

It is now almost four hundred years since that afternoon in 1599 when London playgoers packed into the Curtain Playhouse in Shoreditch (or perhaps the newly completed Globe Theatre on Bankside) to watch the first performance of *Henry V*. As a result, for nearly four centuries people have been able to comment on, discuss, argue over and debate the nature and quality of Shakespeare's achievement, and if only a fraction of that mass of remarks and observations has appeared in written form and is thereby accessible today, it still constitutes a formidable body of material, too vast to be adequately covered in a volume this size. All it has been possible to do is to explore *Henry V* from a number of angles, in the hope that this will illuminate the play sufficiently to enable readers and spectators to define and develop opinions of their own. These concluding remarks should therefore not be viewed as an attempt to supply a 'final verdict' on the play, but rather as an attempt to re-formulate some of the issues discussed already and to present them for further consideration.

Writing in an Oxford magazine just after World War II had ended, the late Kenneth Tynan observed that 'this sad age needs to be dazzled, shaped, and spurred by the spectacle of heroism . . . If heroic plays take the stage, life may produce, in honest emulation, its own poor heroes of flesh and fact.' In a sense this may still be seen as one justification for the presentation of *Henry V*, or at least of Olivier's film version of it, which I began this short study by invoking. Henry as a dramatic character seems tailored to suit times when the national morale is at a low ebb, and we have already seen how Shakespeare's play has often been called on to act as a beacon of hope at seasons of crisis in his country's fortunes. But it is notable that in order to sustain such a bland reading parts of the text always have to be jettisoned; thus Olivier's textual adviser, Alan Dent, cut away such embarrassing elements as the Cambridge–Scroop–Grey conspiracy, Henry's speech threatening the citizens of Harfleur and the massacre of the French prisoners at Agincourt, Bardolph's execution and the awkward question of regal responsibility posed by Williams, all of which omissions helped to sustain the image of the all-gracious king, flawless in chivalry.

Not that we should necessarily condemn that strong streak of ruthlessness and pragmatism which Shakespeare brings out in Henry's make-up; are we to regard conciliatory or concessive tactics as a strength or a

Conclusion

weakness in a great war-leader? Sixteenth-century standards are not ours, and yet on this matter many citizens of late twentieth-century Britain might endorse their Tudor predecessors' predilection for firm government and determined leadership if they felt that the nation's future was at stake. On the other hand, others may not be able to resist invoking to Henry's detriment George Orwell's useful distinction between patriotism and nationalism, which runs thus:

> By 'patriotism' I mean devotion to a particular place and a particular way of life, which one believes to be the best in the world but has no wish to force upon other people. Patriotism is of its nature defensive, both militarily and culturally. Nationalism, on the other hand, is inseparable from the desire for power. The abiding purpose of every nationalist is to secure more power and more prestige, *not* for himself but for the nation or other unit in which he has chosen to sink his own individuality.
>
> 'Notes on Nationalism', 1945

Does Orwell's description of nationalism not fit Shakespeare's portrayal of Henry far better than does his definition of patriotism?

By such a reckoning Henry V is not a model for our times any more than Coriolanus or Petruchio is, yet even those who feel that they can forgive Shakespeare for making a military conqueror his apparent hero still sense that what they regard as the lack of character conflict (both internal and external) is fatal to dramatic success. We have already considered whether or not there is anything like dramatic development or tension in Henry as Shakespeare presents him, but for many people the play's success does not seem to depend on the amount of interest Henry's character generates. In the study he can seem static and flat, but as most spectators would agree, the case is very much altered in the theatre. There Henry's apparent lack of psychological progression, the apparent absence of much complexity in his personality worries us very little: we do not expect to have Henry's secret self exposed or explored, as if Shakespeare were some investigative Sunday journalist about to shock us with unexpected revelations. As we have seen, modern critics have been able to equip the king with a very convincing selection of Achilles heels, but it can scarcely be maintained that Shakespeare has composed a penetrating portrait of a man with a split personality. In the two hours' traffic of the stage the negative aspects are usually muted.

What matters more at this juncture is the question of the play's true quality. Dramatic excellence does not depend on the degree of complexity which a play possesses; indeed, some dramas sink beneath the weight of their own complications, either of plot or argument. Drama must

Masterstudies: Henry V

necessarily simplify issues and characters by its very nature, and a play is not necessarily the worse for being streamlined. Yet a number of critics have felt *Henry V* to be among the least satisfactory of its author's compositions; in 1908 Sir Sidney Lee argued that the piece was:

> as far as possible removed from what is generally understood by drama. It is without intrigue or entanglement; it propounds no problems of psychology; its definite motive is neither comic nor tragic; women play in it the slenderest part; it lacks plot in any customary sense...

and he was echoed a few years later by John Masefield in less respectful terms:

> The play bears every mark of having been hastily written. Though it belongs to the great period of Shakespeare's creative life, it contains little either of clash of character, or of that much tamer thing, comparison of character. It is a chronicle or procession, eked out with soldiers' squabbles. It seems to have been written to fill a gap in the series of the historical plays...
>
> *Shakespeare*, 1911

To such adverse opinions of the play's merits one can most fitly reply perhaps by quoting Robert Ornstein once again:

> More critics are willing to defend the character of Henry V than to defend the play that bears his name. Those who admire *Henry V* as a rousing patriotic spectacle do not make many claims for it as a work of dramatic art. Those who regard it as a falling off from the History Plays that preceded it declare that it is a complaisant if not shallow play, somewhat simplistic in its subject matter and a bit brassy in its enthusiasms. Some even suggest that Shakespeare was not deeply engaged by or interested in the play, that he probably felt compelled to write it to complete his tetralogy or to satisfy his audience's desire for the heroic story of Agincourt. What evidence is there, however, that *Henry V* was work of the left hand? Little in it is perfunctory or indifferent; it has none of the muddles and contradictions of *King John*, none of the lapses of inspiration that are obvious in other History Plays. The poetry is always more than adequate to its dramatic purpose; the characterizations are lively and interesting if not fully developed; and the plot is very skillfully contrived and varied in mood and pace...

As we have already observed, the play may not present the panoramic sweep which its predecessors in the historical sequence, *1 and 2 Henry IV*, deploy with such assurance, and it may lack the intensity of vision by which *Richard II* is able to invest the confrontation between Bolingbroke and Richard with resonances, but *Henry V* has its own dimension of easy directness and enigmatic indirection intermingled, so that our response ceases to be as predictable as that play's reputation might suggest. Some may wish to argue that a drama which can be interpreted in at least two mutually contradictory ways must be inferior

Conclusion

to one in which the basic level of significance is not in dispute, but by now the existence of a plurality of interpretations has surely become the hallmark of those major works of art which continue to reveal fresh layers of meaning as year succeeds to year. As Norman Rabkin wisely observes in the article quoted from on an earlier page: '... if we do not try obsessively to cling to memories of past encounters with the play, we may find that each time we read it it turns from one shape to another, just as it so regularly does in production.' While it may not have generated so much critical discussion as many other works in the canon, *Henry V* is no less capable of becoming the subject of vigorous debate, among scholars and 'common readers' and spectators.

Yet a slight impression of disappointment must perhaps be the inevitable accompaniment to a reading or a viewing of this play, perhaps because we have become over-accustomed to being granted some kind of privileged intimacy with the heroes of Shakespeare's major dramas. Only rarely do we share Henry's personal thoughts and emotions, as we do those of Richard II or Hamlet, Macbeth or Antony: Shakespeare rarely allows Henry to be seen without his public mask firmly in place. In this sense we may feel that the play cheats us of our legitimate rights, but if so, we really do need to be re-educated into the function and methods of theatre. We are perhaps too prone to regard Elizabethan and Jacobean drama as predominantly a confessional mode, accustomed as we are to receiving the confidences of a Faustus, an Iago, a Volpone. By contrast, the one glimpse we have of Henry's private self is quickly over, and we thereafter find ourselves ceasing to sort the 'real' human individual from the role he plays so effectively and purposefully.

There is also the sense of anticlimax which many people receive from the somewhat tame presentation of the battle itself, and the fifth act as a whole when, as Ornstein remarks, 'the glow of Agincourt begins to fade'. The justification for the lack of military action does not have to carry sinister overtones for those who prefer to see Agincourt as a notable victory: the Chorus has assured the audience that 'four or five most vile and ragged foils' will be deployed to create a pallid representation of the battlefield, and there is no reason to believe that this was not done in production. The fact that no lines exist in the text to accompany this token warfare does not mean to say that fighting did not take place on stage between scenes or even while dialogue was being exchanged on another part of the platform. No modern director worth his salt omits any kind of combat other than that indicated in the encounter between Pistol and his French prisoner, and there is no need to assume that the original production as conceived by Shakespeare would have sought to deprive Henry of his finest hour, or audiences of the sight of some physical scrapping.

Masterstudies: Henry V

The play's fifth act is not much to modern taste, and we have to make the best of it. Victory at Agincourt would have made a firm conclusion in one sense, and yet it would suggest that the play was simply about a military expedition and nothing else. A total victory is an inspiring thing, however much we may deplore the barbarism and horrors of war, but had Shakespeare ended with Henry's slightly self-satisfied lines which conclude Act IV, there would have been a hollowness at the heart of things which would have justified all the anti-jingoists' derogatory assertions. But as an audience we wish to see what the upshot of this famous triumph is to be, not simply for Henry and his cause, but also for the other participants. As I said earlier, many of our hopes are frustrated – several characters do not make a reappearance – but at least in the case of Pistol, Fluellen and Gower, the opportunity is created to show the braggart hoist with his own petard, and yet not much the worse for his humiliation. The recalcitrant element is not to be fully assimilated into the new regime of peace and plenty.

Moreover, without the final scene of the play, one might still be in doubt as to the attitude the play adopts towards military conquest. Henry may be the victor, but Burgundy's great speech on the breach which war makes in the face of nature is made to carry a good deal of weight in the context of the peace talks upon which the rival monarchs are about to embark. Warfare may be endowed with its own virtues and rewards, but Burgundy feelingly persuades us of its essential limitations as a mode of human expression, and extols with all the eloquence his creator can muster the merits of peace and the blessedness of peacemakers. Shakespeare is honest enough to recognize that conflict and danger can bring out our communal talent for comradeship, cheerfulness in adversity and courage, and to admit that aggression and acquisitiveness are as much part of our human nature as altruism and acquiescence. Yet, while the Elizabethans may have viewed too long a period of peace as risky for the nation's physical and moral fibre, there is no reason to assume that they regarded the remorseless pursuit of war as axiomatic, or any cessation of hostilities as cowardly or effete. Even if they did so, it seems clear that Burgundy's measured speech carries no such connotations. In his memorable plea for the re-establishment of a world released from the scourge of war, we find perhaps the final justification for the fifth act of *Henry V*. This king may have been presented to us as a famous military hero in whom there is more to be admired than deplored, but his most notable achievement is surely to be regarded not as the work of Henry, the winner of a notable battle, but of Henry, the willing participator in a long overdue peace.

Further Reading

Texts

At least one of the following paperback editions should be studied: *The Arden Shakespeare*, ed. J. H. Walter, London, 1954; *The Signet Classic Shakespeare*, ed. John Russell Brown, New York and London, 1965; *The New Penguin Shakespeare*, ed. A. R. Humphreys, Harmondsworth, 1968; *The Oxford Shakespeare*, ed. Gary Taylor, Oxford, 1982. (All quotations and references in this study are taken from the Penguin edition.)

The introductions to the New Penguin and the Oxford editions can be warmly recommended as can the notes to the Arden and the Oxford texts; the Arden introduction now seems too tersely one-sided, but is informative. The Oxford text, which relies heavily on the First Quarto, may occasionally puzzle those familiar with the more usual versions, or unfamiliar with Taylor's arguments in support of his approach.

History and the Elizabethans

Several works cited below, under 'The Play', will be found useful, but note the comments made there: debate has often concentrated on how far Shakespeare echoes the political orthodoxies of his time. Two articles in *English Studies* 55 (1974) typify the many sceptical responses to the notion: R. E. Burkhart, 'Obedience and Rebellion in Shakespeare's Early History Plays' (pp. 108–17) and A. L. French, 'The Mills of God and Shakespeare's Early History Plays' (pp. 313–24). Two very valuable broader discussions are A. R. Humphreys, 'Shakespeare and the Tudor Perception of History' in *Shakespeare Celebrated*, ed. Louis B. Wright, New York, 1966, and J. W. Lever, 'Shakespeare and the Ideas of his Time', *Shakespeare Survey* 29 (1976), pp. 79–91. More recent claims that Shakespeare's work embodies more radical and subversive attitudes are typified in Jonathan Dollimore, *Radical Tragedy*, Brighton, 1984; see also *Alternative Shakespeares*, ed. John Drakakis, London, 1985 (see particularly Jonathan Dollimore and Alan Sinfield, 'History and Ideology: The Instance of *Henry V*', pp. 206–27); James Siemon, *Shakespeare's Iconoclasm*, Berkeley, 1985, especially pp. 100–13.

The Historical Henry

The standard account is still J. H. Wylie, *The Reign of Henry the Fifth*, 3 vols., Cambridge, 1914–29, but most readers will prefer either Harold F. Hutchinson, *Henry V: A Biography*, London, 1967, or Peter Earle, *The Life and Times of Henry V*, London, 1972, both lively modern biographies. Also to be recommended are John Harvey, *The Plantagenets*, London, 1948, and K. B. Macfarlane, 'Henry V:

Masterstudies: Henry V

A Personal Portrait' in his *Lancastrian Kings and Lollard Knights*, Oxford, 1972, pp. 114–33. For the relevant portions of Holinshed and other contemporary accounts, see *Narrative and Dramatic Sources of Shakespeare*, ed. Geoffrey Bullough, 8 vols., London, 1957–75, vol. IV, pp. 347–432.

Henry V Plays

The text of *The Famous Victories* is found in Bullough, vol. IV, pp. 299–343, where the extract from *Tarlton's Jests* is also printed on pp. 289–90. Nashe's *Pierce Penilesse* will be found in full in *The Works of Thomas Nashe*, ed. Ronald B. McKerrow, 5 vols., London, 1904–10, reprinted Oxford, 1958; vol. I, pp. 137–245. The Arden editions of *1 Henry IV* and *2 Henry IV*, edited by A. R. Humphreys, contain much useful information on the relationship between this group of historical dramas

Shakespeare and War

The most thorough and consistently interesting treatment of this topic remains Paul A. Jorgensen's *Shakespeare's Military World*, Berkeley, 1956, from which many of my illustrations have been taken; also valuable from the factual angle is C. B. Cruickshank, *Elizabeth's Army*, Oxford, 1946. For a succinct survey of English military commitments in the latter part of the century, see G. B. Harrison, 'The National Background' in *A Companion to Shakespeare Studies*, eds. Harley Granville-Barker and G. B. Harrison, Cambridge, 1934, pp. 163 86. For a vivid picture of the nation's vulnerable position in 1588, it is a pleasure to recommend Garrett Mattingly's *The Defeat of the Spanish Armada*, London, 1959.

The Play

Unlike many of Shakespeare's dramas, *Henry V* is rarely treated in isolation (as far as books are concerned, at all events), and it is more usual to find it dealt with as one of Shakespeare's history plays, or in conjunction with *Richard II* and the two parts of *Henry IV* with which it is sometimes said to form 'the second tetralogy'. Among the best books in one or both of these fields the following seem to be worth recommending:

- E. M. W. Tillyard, *Shakespeare's History Plays*, London, 1944 (full of insights, if dismissive of *Henry V*; marred by its determination to see the plays as supporting the tenets of Tudor absolutism)
- Lily B. Campbell, *Shakespeare's 'Histories': Mirrors of Tudor Policy*, San Marino, 1947 (valuable material, but limited, as its title suggests, notably by its insistence on the concept of divine retribution)
- Derek A. Traversi, *Shakespeare from 'Richard II' to 'Henry V'*, London, 1957 (a convincingly close account of the development of Shakespeare's perception of the political process at work in English history; thoughtful on *Henry V*)

Further Reading

Irving Ribner, *The English History Play in the Age of Shakespeare*, Princeton, 1957, rev. ed., 1965 (mainly a 'background book', which concerns itself chiefly with the nature of the history play)

S. C. Sen Gupta, *Shakespeare's Historical Plays*, Oxford, 1964 (sees Shakespeare as interested in people rather than politics)

H. M. Richmond, *Shakespeare's Political Plays*, New York, 1967 (an intelligent assessment of the complexities within the history plays)

Henry Ansgar Kelly, *Divine Providence in the England of Shakespeare's Histories*, Cambridge, Mass., 1970 (despite its clumsy title, an excellent, well-documented work, refuting the Tillyard Campbell thesis of support for established orthodoxy)

Robert Ornstein, *A Kingdom for a Stage*, Cambridge, Mass., 1972 (just possibly the 'best book'; a sustained analysis of the critical debate and a shrewd assessment of Shakespeare's approach to historical materials)

Moody E. Prior, *The Dream of Power*, Evanston, Ill., 1973 (stresses the individuality of the plays but relates them to Elizabethan political thought)

H. R. Coursen, *The Leasing Out of England: Shakespeare's Second Henriad*, Washington, DC, 1982 (influenced by knowledge of Tudor economic problems)

Many works which deal exclusively with the figure of Henry concentrate on his youthful escapades, his conversion from playboy to monarch and the rejection of Falstaff, all of which are more suitable for inclusion in a bibliography for *Henry IV*. Of those which focus on the hero of *Henry V* the majority are articles in scholarly journals; listed below are a few of the more provocative and noteworthy of the recent articles (some earlier items are printed in the collections by Michael Quinn and Ronald Berman, cited below):

Roy Battenhouse, '*Henry V* as Heroic Comedy' in *Essays on Shakespeare and Elizabethan Drama...*, ed. Richard Hosley, Columbia, Mo, 1963, pp. 163 82; C. H. Hobday, 'Imagery and Irony in *Henry V*', *Shakespeare Survey* 21 (1968), pp. 107 113; Anne Barton, 'The King Disguised: Shakespeare's *Henry V* and the Comical History', in *The Triple Bond*, ed. Joseph G. Price, Pennsylvania, 1975, pp. 92 117; Karl P. Wentersdorf, 'The Conspiracy of Silence in *Henry V*', *Shakespeare Quarterly* 27 (1976), pp. 264 87; Gordon Ross Smith, 'Shakespeare's *Henry V*: Another Part of the Critical Forest', *Journal of the History of Ideas* 37 (1976), pp. 3 26; William Babula, 'Whatever Happened to Prince Hal?' *Shakespeare Survey* 30 (1977), pp. 47 59; Andrew Gurr, '*Henry V* and the Bees' Commonwealth', ibid., pp. 61 72; Norman Rabkin, 'Rabbits, Ducks and *Henry V*', *Shakespeare Quarterly* 28 (1977), pp. 279 96; Brownell Salomon, 'Thematic Contraries and the Dramaturgy of *Henry V*', *Shakespeare Quarterly* 31 (1980), pp. 343 56; Paul Dean, 'Chronicle and Romance Mode in *Henry V*', *Shakespeare Quarterly* 32 (1981), pp. 18–27.

Mention must also be made of excellent surveys of available materials on the Histories, by Harold Jenkins in *Shakespeare Survey* 6 (1953), which covers the years 1900–51, and by Dennis H. Burden in *Shakespeare Survey* 38 (1985), for the

Masterstudies: Henry V

period 1952–83. Two anthologies of selected criticism will also be found useful: Michael Quinn's Casebook (1969) contains extracts from (among others) Hazlitt, Masefield, Tillyard, Van Doren and Sprague, as well as part of Gerald Gould's 'A New Reading of *Henry V*' (1919); Charles Williams's eulogy of 1936; Rose A. Zimbardo, 'The Formalism of *Henry V*' (1964) and Zdenek Stribrny, '*Henry V* and History', first published in *Shakespeare in a Changing World*, ed. Arnold Kettle, London and New York, 1964. Ronald Berman's *Twentieth Century Interpretations of 'Henry V'* includes extracts from Lily B. Campbell, Bullough's introduction, Tillyard, Williams's essay, Traversi, A. P. Rossiter's iconoclastic 'Ambivalence: The Dialectic of the Histories' from *Angel With Horns*, London and New York, 1961, and M. M. Reese's helpful survey, *The Cease of Majesty*, London and New York, 1961, as well as snippets from others, including Jorgensen's *Shakespeare's Military World*, which is worth fuller exposure.

The Play in the Theatre

General surveys which deal with *Henry V* where appropriate include George C. D. Odell, *Shakespeare from Betterton to Irving*, 2 vols., London, 1920; reprinted New York, 1963 (old-fashioned in some of its attitudes, but full of data); A. C. Sprague, *Shakespeare's Histories: Plays for the Stage*, London, 1964 (a chapter on productions of *Henry* occupies pp. 92–110); J. C. Trewin, *Shakespeare on the English Stage, 1900–1964*, London, 1964 (useful broad survey with good pictures); Robert Speaight, *Shakespeare on the Stage*, London, 1973 (includes US and Continental productions, with excellent colour illustrations). For specific productions, see Audrey Williamson, *Old Vic Drama*, London, 1948 (for the 1937 Guthrie/Olivier venture); J. D. Wilson and T. C. Worsley, *Shakespeare's Histories at Stratford, 1951*, New York, 1952 (Burton's first Hal and Henry V); Richard David, *Shakespeare in the Theatre*, Cambridge, 1978, for the Stratford production of 1975, which is also chronicled in *The Royal Shakespeare Company's Production of Henry V*, ed. Sally Beauman, Oxford, 1976. These can be supplemented with reviews and notices, especially from *The Times*, the *Daily Telegraph*, the (*Manchester*) *Guardian*, the *Sunday Times*, the *Observer*, the *Listener*, the *New Statesman*, the *Spectator* etc., as well as *Shakespeare Quarterly* and *Shakespeare Survey*, and from such biographies as J. C. Trewin, *Benson and the Bensonians*, London, 1960 and Paul Ferris, *Richard Burton*, London, 1981.

Study Aids

Henry V is available on disc, cassette, film and video recording.

FOR THE BEST IN PAPERBACKS, LOOK FOR THE 🐧

In every corner of the world, on every subject under the sun, Penguin represents quality and variety – the very best in publishing today.

For complete information about books available from Penguin – including Pelicans, Puffins, Peregrines and Penguin Classics – and how to order them, write to us at the appropriate address below. Please note that for copyright reasons the selection of books varies from country to country.

In the United Kingdom: For a complete list of books available from Penguin in the U.K., please write to *Dept E.P., Penguin Books Ltd, Harmondsworth, Middlesex, UB7 0DA*

In the United States: For a complete list of books available from Penguin in the U.S., please write to *Dept BA, Penguin, 299 Murray Hill Parkway, East Rutherford, New Jersey 07073*

In Canada: For a complete list of books available from Penguin in Canada, please write to *Penguin Books Canada Ltd, 2801 John Street, Markham, Ontario L3R 1B4*

In Australia: For a complete list of books available from Penguin in Australia, please write to the *Marketing Department, Penguin Books Australia Ltd, P.O. Box 257, Ringwood, Victoria 3134*

In New Zealand: For a complete list of books available from Penguin in New Zealand, please write to the *Marketing Department, Penguin Books (NZ) Ltd, Private Bag, Takapuna, Auckland 9*

In India: For a complete list of books available from Penguin, please write to *Penguin Overseas Ltd, 706 Eros Apartments, 56 Nehru Place, New Delhi, 110019*

In Holland: For a complete list of books available from Penguin in Holland, please write to *Penguin Books Nederland B.V., Postbus 195, NL–1380AD Weesp, Netherlands*

In Germany: For a complete list of books available from Penguin, please write to *Penguin Books Ltd, Friedrichstrasse 10 – 12, D–6000 Frankfurt Main 1, Federal Republic of Germany*

In Spain: For a complete list of books available from Penguin in Spain, please write to *Longman Penguin España, Calle San Nicolas 15, E–28013 Madrid, Spain*